SOUS VIDE

THE ART OF PRECISION COOKING

www.sousvidetools.com

Duck Supreme

SOUS VIDE COOKING CAN LOOK RARER THAN YOU'RE USED TO...

...but it's perfectly cooked.

Acknowledgements

Since starting our journey at SousVideTools.com it has been an ambition of ours to create a sous vide cookery book. This was further emphasized by our customers constantly asking us when there would be a sous vide recipe book on the market written by someone from the UK and so we decided to do something about it.

We teamed up with our Development Chef Chris Holland and his sous chef Gary Woolliscroft and got to work. We started by sitting around a table and making notes about the best dishes Chris and Gary had created in their restaurant, some of the best dishes we have eaten around the world and what we love cooking at home.

All of a sudden we had something that started to look like content for a recipe book. So what next? We incorporated the assistance of Matblack, a creative design agency, to come up with the design and styling element of the book. We also called on Mark Carr for the photography.

Chris and Gary got down to creating the wonderfully tasty dishes and Mark started shooting the shots of the food. This was the best job in the world as we got to oversee it all and eat some of the dishes once the photos had been taken — well we didn't want them going to waste.

We are delighted that with the hard work of our colleagues and with the initial push from our customers this cook book has come to life and we hope you enjoy it.

Thanks, the team at SousVideTools.com

Contents

Introduction

The French word *'sous vide'* translates as *'under vacuum'*. It was originally used in the early 1970s to minimise product loss when cooking foie gras. Now it is loved by chefs worldwide for the preparation of many dishes.

Food is vacuum–sealed in a pouch and then cooked slowly at low temperatures. The food becomes tender without losing its original colour, nutrients, and texture.

The technique involves heating foods to the right temperature, for the right length of time. Temperature depends on the kind of food and would vary for meat, fish and vegetables, but also depends on personal taste. For example whether a customer prefers it cooked rare or medium.

SOUS VIDE vs CONVENTIONAL COOKING METHODS

With all cooking techniques heat penetrates the outside of the food until the centre gets to the right temperature. If you wanted a rare piece of beef you would cook the centre to 54°C. To do this you may roast it in an oven at around 180°C. By the time the centre of the beef is at 54°C the outside of the beef is way overdone. In fact most of the joint would be well done and grey.

But if you roasted it at 54°C, none of the meat would get overdone, although it takes so long for the centre to get to the right temperature the meat would dry out. If you stopped roasting too early so it didn't dry out, the centre would still be raw.

With the sous vide technique you cook food at the temperature you want the whole joint to be at. By sealing it in a vacuumed bag, or pouch, none of the meat is overdone or dry, and you keep all the nutrients and flavours.

WHY IS PRECISE TEMPERATURE CONTROL IMPORTANT?

The art of sous vide cooking is finding the perfect core temperature to achieve the desired taste and textures. Think of a dish that features an egg with a creamy, custard–like texture. One chef might cook that egg to a core temperature of 61.7°C, while another may prefer cooking it to 63.3°C. The finished eggs will be very different from each other. It makes each chef's dish unique.

THE SCIENCE

When cooking, the heat induces chemical reactions with different effects at different temperatures. For example, the different proteins in the albumen of eggs coagulate at specific temperatures. Just a few degrees difference in cooking temperature will affect just how much the egg white solidifies.

Temperature affects meat in the same way. Cuts with high collagen content, such as a pork belly, should be cooked for longer and at higher temperatures. This will break down the tough connective tissue. Meat with little connective tissue, like fillet steak, would get tough if cooked at those temperatures. Just a few degrees can make a difference in an expensive cut of meat.

CAN I NOT JUST USE A PAN OF WATER OR SLOW COOKER?

The right equipment is a vital part of the sous vide technique. Unlike slow cookers or simmering pans of water, sous vide equipment offers precise temperature control along with 'set it and forget it' convenience. Basically you set it to cook food to a precise core temperature, within a fraction of a degree, with just one single adjustment.

Maintaining a slow cooker or pan of simmering water at just the right temperature is practically impossible, and it is much harder for results to be consistent. Also, because they don't circulate the cooking liquid, these methods can develop hot and cool zones that affect the cooking process.

HOW DO COOKING TIMES VARY?

Cooking at low temperatures for long periods of time is what creates the delicious results of sous vide. However, it does take testing and experience to determine the right amount of time needed to cook a dish exactly how the customer wants.

The *sousvidetools.com* team can help with this.

In general, cooking time is affected by three factors:

1. The core temperature you wish to cook the dish to,
2. The heat transfer characteristics of the food,
3. The amount of food that will be cooked at one time.

Food will reach the core temperate quicker with a greater cooking liquid to food ratio. When cooking sous vide, the pouches must be completely covered with liquid and you should allow enough room for the pouches and liquid to circulate freely.

One advantage of sous vide cooking is that it's much harder to overcook a dish by leaving it too long. Once a dish reaches the desired temperature, it takes more time to keep cooking the food. This means you can keep it at that temperature for longer without the food shrinking, drying out or becoming tough. This is a great benefit when cooking expensive cuts of meat.

HOW DOES THE SOUS VIDE TECHNIQUE IMPROVE PRESENTATION?

The enjoyment of food is a very personal experience and it must please all our senses. We've all had our expectations raised by the sight of a well-presented dish, the aroma from the plate, or the sizzling sound of a hot meat.

To complement and enhance the melt in the mouth tenderness, many chefs 'finish' sous vide meat dishes by briefly grilling or pan/blowtorch searing. It creates a browning reaction and then the familiar aromas and flavours that come with high–heat cooking.

The main difference with food cooked using the sous vide technique and finished in this way is that the inside remains tender and moist.

HOW TO COOK USING THE SOUS VIDE TECHNIQUE?

The sous vide cooking process is very simple:

1. Set the thermal circulator or water bath to the desired cooking temperature,
2. Vacuum seal the food,
3. Place the vacuum sealed food in the water bath.

The thermal circulator or water bath will maintain the water or oil at the desired temperature.

Note:

While you can't overcook a dish with the sous vide method, you can undercook it if you remove it from the heated liquid before it reaches the right temperature.

VACUUM PACKING IS A METHOD OF PACKAGING, STORING, PRESENTING AND THEN COOKING FOOD...

Some food types need to be stored in an airless environment, usually in air-tight packaging to reduce the growth of micro-organisms. When vacuum packing most of the bacteria is expelled from the bag as the air is removed, providing a very safe and hygienic method of storage.

Vacuum packing also helps maintain the product quality and size. For example, in meat items such as steaks, the blood can't leak out and the meat doesn't dry out so the product weight is maintained. Vacuum packing food can extend its life by three to five times.

WHAT BENEFITS DOES A VACUUM PACKING MACHINE PROVIDE?

Chefs and caterers find many benefits when using vacuum packing machines including:

- Advanced food preparation
- Portion control
- Spreading workload
- Reduced food wastage
- Lower food costs
- Safer food storage
- Higher standards of food hygiene when used together with sous vide cooking

Pre-prepared foods such as fresh or sliced meats, fish, poultry, vegetables, fruits, salads and cheeses can be stored for several days without reduced quality. By pre-portioning soups, sauces and completed dishes you can reduce food wastage.

All these benefits help increase efficiency in the kitchen. Cooked and raw food can be hygienically stocked in vacuum pouches for storage in the fridge or easily transported between locations with minimal risks of cross-contamination.

BENEFITS OF SEALING FOOD UNDER VACUUM.

ELIMINATING OXIDISATION

Vacuum packing helps preserve food by removing air from the bag it is stored in. This gets rid of oxygen which affects food in various ways including odour, colour, taste and texture and allows for longer storage. Certain types of bacteria cannot grow without oxygen. Once food is in contact with air it begins to lose its natural flavour and its appearance starts to change. This reaction affects all fresh foods even if the effects are not immediately obvious.

PRESERVING DELICATE FLAVOURS AND OILS

In today's world a lot of emphasis is placed on eliminating salt and fat from our diets and increasing natural oils. More of us are trying to eat fish which is rich in omega-3 fatty acids as these lower blood levels of triglycerides, which have been linked to cardiovascular disease.

Fish oils do deteriorate faster than the fat found in meat such as beef, chicken and pork. You can keep fish well wrapped in a fridge for two days and in a freezer for two months. By vacuum packing these foods you can preserve all the natural goodness and taste for four to six days in the fridge or frozen for two years.

PREVENTING FREEZER BURN

When foods are frozen without preparation, freezer burn can occur. It happens when the surface of the food is dehydrated and this causes a dried and leathery appearance. The flavour and texture of foods can also be ruined. Vacuum packing reduces freezer burn as it protects the food from exposure to the cold, dry air.

MAINTAINING NATURAL MOISTURE

Air causes moisture to evaporate. One of the reasons we package or wrap food is to keep it from drying out. How many of us reach a few slices down into the loaf of bread to find the softer slices? Vacuum packing is a much better way to pack food because the air removal keeps the food moist.

TOOLS FOR THE JOB

This is a section on the right tools to begin the sous vide journey with the confidence to succeed.

VACUUM POUCHES

Food that is to be cooked sous vide needs to be placed in a vacuum pouch. Vacuum sealer bags can also be used as a method of storing food, which will extend its life by up to five times. The packaging creates an airless environment to prevent food from spoiling. This is achieved by preventing the growth of microorganisms, removing atmospheric oxygen, limiting the growth of aerobic bacteria or fungi and preventing the evaporation of volatile components.

There are three types of vacuum sealer bags:

The first are embossed for domestic/external suction vacuum sealers. These have a criss-crossing pattern in the bag to allow the air to navigate out of the bag successfully.

The second type are smooth for use with chamber vacuum packing machines.

The third type of bags are Zip Lock bags. If you don't have a chamber vacuum packing machine and need to seal food along with a liquid these offer as a handy alternative. Zip lock bags offer the convenience of a zip closure in a bag designed specifically to safely seal foods for both sous vide cooking and storage.

Please ensure when buying vacuum pouches that they are suitable for sous vide cooking, as some brands are not and the pouches material can break down and the pouch will fall apart during the cooking process.

VACUUM PACKING MACHINES

Vacuum Packing is a very modern way to keep food fresh. Food that is to be cooked sous vide does have to be vacuum packed first. This is for two reasons. The first is that foods will fall apart if left unwrapped in the bath. The second is that air-filled bags float on the top of the water. This is dangerous as the food may not be cooked all of the way through.

There are two types of machine available for both the home and professional market. At SousVideTools we offer both types. The first are external suction vacuum sealers that use a vacuum pump to suck air out of a pouch from the exterior of the appliance, i.e. by placing the open end of the pouch underneath a lid, withdrawing the air and then heat sealing the pouch. The only drawback to these machines is that they are not designed to be used with any kind of liquid product as the vacuum pump will get damaged. Any liquid would be sucked out of the bag at the same time as the air. The second type are chamber vacuum packing machines that create a vacuum in a pouch by placing the entire contents of a pouch within a chamber and extracting the air from the chamber before heat sealing the pouch. These machines are designed for use with liquids. In some circumstances it is better to use an external vacuum sealer machine such as in the home where space is at a premium and budgets are more restrictive.

WATER BATHS

Needless to say you will need a sous vide machine to complete the cooking process. Fortunately we work with the world's leading brands so have made some suggestions here. Water Baths come in two varieties, stirred and non–stirred. Non-stirred water baths rely on convection where hot fluids rise and cold fluids sink, causing the water to gently circulate. Circulating water baths are becoming more and more popular among both the home and professional chef. These are called Sous Vide Thermal Circulators. These machines are a standalone device that are simply mounted on any vessel such as a stock pot by using its attachment clamp thus turning the container into a water bath. These machines circulate and heat the water at a more accurate and stable temperature than a non-stirred water bath. As the water is stirred by a pump at an average of 6 litres a minute they eliminate the risk of hot and cold spots. The benefit of a thermal circulator is its adaptability to be attached to different sizes of container dependent on your cooking needs. For example, cooking for two the thermal circulator could be attached to a small 5 litre stock pot or to a cool box when cooking for 15 at a dinner party.

SousVideTools.com work with the world's leading brands of sous vide and vacuum packing equipment for the home cook and professional chef including SousVide Supreme, PolyScience and Foodtek. To see the best solution for your application please feel free to contact us via our website, or you can call us for more information on **0800 678 5001.**

FOOD SAFETY

As with any food process, sous vide requires specified food handling practices to prevent, eliminate, or reduce the food biological, chemical, and physical hazards to a safe level.

Three important aspects require additional attention:

1. When food is vacuum packed Vacuum-packaged food creates an anaerobic (oxygen-free) or reduced oxygen environment. With improper food handling, some of the most dangerous bacteria can grow, such as salmonella and botulism. Safe food handling and hygiene standards should always be maintained.

2. Food cooked at low temperatures for extended periods of time can cause bacteria to multiply rapidly. The longer food is in the 'danger zone' — temperatures between 4.4°C to 60°C — the faster bacteria can multiply and the more dangerous they can become.

3. When food in the pouch has finished the required cooking time, it has to be removed and served immediately, or rapidly chilled. Cooling must be less than 3°C within 90 minutes.

SOUS VIDE PROCESSING STEP-BY-STEP

The basic steps of the sous vide process are shown below.

Prepare the work area. Put away unnecessary objects. Clean and sanitise food contact surfaces, and store chemicals so that they cannot contaminate the food.

Get fresh ingredients. Sous vide cannot make spoiled ingredients taste good. It amplifies the flavours and should only be applied to the freshest ingredients.

Trim, cut and prepare ingredients. Remember, the thicker the protein ingredient, the longer it takes to come to its cooking temperature. Less than 2 inch thickness is a practical maximum thickness. Weigh additives carefully. Safe cook times can be calculated in PolyScience iPhone/iPad app "Sous Vide Toolbox".

Package/vacuum seal. The purpose of the vacuum is to pull the plastic pouch film tight to the food for good heat transfer. Check the seal.

Cook/pasteurise. Reduce vegetative pathogens such as Salmonella 5 log (100,000 to 1). Cooking/pasteurisation begins about 54.5 °C.

Hold at cooking temperature until desired degree of doneness is achieved.

Cool fast enough to prevent the outgrowth of spores (less than 3°C within 90 minutes).

Cold hold meat, poultry, and vegetables at 5ºC to prevent the outgrowth of spores and slow growth of spoilage organisms.

Warm (reheating) and serve.

IS COOKING IN PLASTIC BAGS SAFE?

The chief concerns raised about cooking in plastic bags involve the leaching of potentially harmful chemicals, such as BPA (bisphenol-A) and phthalates, or toxic metals, such as lead, from the bag into the food. Food grade plastic bags, certified as suitable for cooking by their manufacturer, are safe to use. All our Vacuum sealer bags have been third-party tested and are certified free of BPA, phthalates and lead.

IF THE FOOD IS SEALED IN PLASTIC, IS THERE ANY MESS TO CLEAN UP?

Clean up couldn't be easier when cooking sous vide. Since the food is sealed in cooking pouches, the water and bath stay clean. Simply toss out the cooking pouch or rinse and recycle in accordance with your communities' standards. As to cleaning the machine itself, once cooking is complete, turn off and unplug the unit, allow the water bath to cool for safety, then simply empty the water from the bath into the sink, and wipe with a dry soft cloth. Occasionally, a cooking pouch may leak if not properly sealed. If this happens, simply remove the cooking pouches, turn off the machine and unplug it. Allow the water to cool, then empty the water and wipe out the interior with mild soap and water. Fill the bath with clean water and empty again. Dry with a clean soft cloth. Do not immerse the machine in water or other liquid.

IS COOKING AT LOW TEMPERATURES SAFE?

Reducing the risk of food-borne illness by cooking food depends not just on temperature, but also on time. The lower the temperature, the longer the time. For instance, Salmonella, a common type of food-borne bacteria, will be killed in 30 seconds at 65.5°C but it will take 15 minutes to do so at 54.5°C. Almost all potentially harmful organisms will be killed at 54.5°C given sufficient time to heat the food completely to that temperature. Since most sous vide cooking is done between 54.5°C and 95°C, the food will be safe. The most common exception is fish, which some people prefer to eat rare or medium rare 46.5°C to 52°C. In this case, it is important to only buy fish you would be willing to eat raw — in other words, sushi grade ocean fish.

HOW DO I MINIMISE MY RISK OF BOTULISM AND OTHER FOOD BORNE DISEASES WHEN COOKING SOUS VIDE?

When handling food, whether cooking sous vide or using more traditional techniques, all cooks should familiarise themselves with basic food safety practices:

1. Make sure food is fresh, high quality and thoroughly cleaned.
2. Don't cross contaminate — use separate cutting boards and storage units for different food, such as vegetables, fish, fruit, poultry, and meat.
3. Properly cook all food. Most bacteria are killed at 54.5°C, and most sous vide cooking temperatures are higher than that, but it's a matter of both temperature and time.
4. Serve food right away or follow proper storage and chilling practices, so that food is not left out at unsafe temperatures.
5. For additional food safety and handling tips, we recommend visiting an approved food safety site such as *www.food.gov.uk*

TAKING CORE TEMPERATURES

To take a temperature inside a vacuum packed pouch you can place special foam tape on the pouch, this will ensure that the vacuum pressure is not lost if the pouch is pierced with a fine needle temperature probe. Your equipment/packaging supplier should be able to provide you with further information. Alternatively you can take a core temperature by opening one of the vacuum packed pouches. If the food does not reach the required core temperatures you must verify your safe methods, this could include further cooking processes or microbiological sampling.

HOW LONG CAN YOU KEEP SOUS VIDE COOKED FOODS IN THE REFRIGERATOR SAFELY?

Food cooked sous vide can be safely kept in the refrigerator for up to 48 hours. To be kept longer, the food should be quick chilled in its pouch and can then be frozen for up to a year.

HOW DO YOU QUICK CHILL SOUS VIDE COOKED FOODS?

Note:

Children, elderly and expectant mothers and those with compromised immune systems should not consume raw or undercooked foods.

To safely refrigerate or freeze food cooked sous vide and not intended for immediate consumption, it should be quick chilled in its cooking pouch, completely submerged in an ice water bath or blast chiller to allow the temperature to drop quickly through the danger zone (less than 3°C within 90 minutes).

Cooking from this book

Both chefs and home cooks would often say the best bit about sous vide is the opportunity to experiment with times, temperatures, seasoning and the addition of flavours to the pouch to ensure the food is cooked exactly to their liking. The excitement of knowing that half a degree and a sprig of herbs made all the difference is one of the great things about it, and we have put the book together to allow you to be able to experiment whilst still having lots of guidance and suggestions.

Each recipe is based around the core product within it, whether that is meat, fish or vegetables and the sous vide times and temperatures to achieve our perfect finish. We have then given a dish suggestion and chef's tip, these aren't designed to be prescriptive and the most important thing is you are having fun and cooking something you enjoy. At the start of the book we have many different brines, cures, butters and marinades that will sit beautifully with many of the dishes. Hopefully this will get your creativity flowing as to what you would like to do and if you want to present the dishes we have suggested then that's great — you won't be disappointed.

Another point to mention is the regeneration times, you will see that many of the dishes take a long slow cook, but the beauty of sous vide is you can cook your dishes in advance, chill in an ice bath and keep in the fridge. Then when you need them they only need to come back up to core temperature which in most instances takes between 20 to 30 minutes.

So for instance, with the Pork Cheeks these could be happily cooking away for twelve hours on their first cook but if you quick chill them after cooking and pop in the fridge you can look forward to serving them in 25 minutes when you next need them. Perfect for chefs to have consistently cooked product on hand for service and for home cooks to batch cook when planning for the week ahead.

Look out for this symbol.

Sous Vide cooking is all about experimentation and the times and temperatures shown within the recipes are our recommendations for the sizes and cuts of meat used.

If you are unsure of any times or temperatures for the sizes and cuts of meat that you have, please see the handy guidelines at the back of this book to help you on your way.

Compressions, Brining, Smoking, Curing, Butters, Pickling and Marinades.

What is compression?

Compression is the process of removing the air from around and inside food — fruit in particular is good to use. When compressed the cell walls are ruptured or *broken* and the air is taken out of the fruit, but not allowed back in when the chamber is released.

The juices from the *broken* fruit fill in the gaps where the air was, giving enhanced flavours, colour and texture.

Flavour
The fruit once compressed doesn't gain flavour from itself — it appears to be more flavour-full because of the absence of air, due to its cell walls being broken down. However, if the compressed fruit was an apple paired with a syrup or pickling liquor, then this liquid would fill the places where air was — the result, a tasty flavour combination.

Colour
The colour change of any fruit compressed is obvious and a delightful improvement from it's raw state, giving the illusion that it has been coloured when it has not. Again this happens because the breakdown of the cell walls releases the fruits natural juices.

Texture
Texture change can give the impression that it has been achieved through cooking using heat just like the colour change. A lot of fruit will change from a raw form to a denser almost cooked state but packed full of flavour.

What is brining?

In cooking, brining is very similar to marination. The meat or fish soak in a solution of salt and sugar — plus spices — with water or wine in some instances for anything up to 12 hours. The amount of time depending on the size of the produce. Similar to curing, brining will help the meat/fish retain moisture when cooked providing an even more succulent finish — it will also impart seasoning and flavour.

What is smoking?

People really enjoy the flavour of smoked produce, and by using the sous vide method, together with the PolyScience smoking gun, this can be achieved relatively easily in the home environment.

Simple equipment needed for smoking would be an air tight plastic container large enough to fit the produce inside, a PolyScience smoking gun and the desired wood chips.

There are many styles of wood chip to use with the smoking process from Beech to Whisky Barrel and Applewood, each giving a subtle difference in flavour.

What is curing?

Curing has been around since ancient times, designed initially to prevent meat and fish from discolouring and giving produce a longer shelf life.

A mixture of salt (or sodium chloride) and sugar are the two main ingredients for the curing process and together they're used to firm up produce and draw out any excess moisture from the meat or fish.

In addition to the sugar in some cases you may use a honey, corn syrup or maple syrup which will add a new flavour dynamic — try Maple Cured Pork Belly.

In most instances the principle use of curing is to firm up produce and provide a better depth of seasoning, enabling you to create real flavour before applying the sous vide method — you'll notice some really amazing results.

Compressions

Pickled Compressed Apple

INGREDIENTS

2 Grannysmith apples

200ml Pickling Liquor — see *pickling* — alternatively use cider or apple juice

METHOD

1. Peel the apple and slice thinly, cutting around the core.

2. Place the slices in a pouch with the pickling liquor.

3. Place in vac pack machine and compress to full bar.

4. Remove one board from the machine just so any liquid doesn't escape during compression. Vacuum compress until the time runs out, remove the bag from machine and reserve in the fridge until needed.

You can also allow 15 to 20 minutes for the colour to become translucent and then use straightaway.

— Dish Suggestion —

Pork Cheek, Pickled Apple, Sage and Onion Mash.

Compressed Pineapple

INGREDIENTS

2 Pineapples

300ml Rum

100g Sugar

4 Star Anise

½ Cinnamon stick

METHOD

1. Peel the pineapple and cut into quarters lengthways, remove the core.

2. Slice thinly or dice 1cm cubes

3. Make a syrup with the rum, star anise, sugar and cinnamon.

4. Cool the syrup and add to a pouch with the pineapple.

5. Compress for 90 seconds and reserve in the fridge.

You can also allow 15 to 20 minutes for full infusion and then use straightaway.

— Dish Suggestion —

Compressed Pineapple with Blue Cheese and Parmesan Crackling.

Compressed Strawberry

INGREDIENTS

1 Punnet (200g) fresh strawberries

200ml Sparkling wine

1 tsp Sugar

METHOD

1. Slice strawberries thinly and place in a pouch.

2. Make a syrup with the sugar and sparkling wine by simmering the ingredients together for 5 minutes.

3. Cool the syrup down and add to the pouch — vac-seal and compress for 99 seconds.

4. Remove from vac-sealer and allow 10 to 20 minutes for infusion.

5. Use straight away or use in within 24 hours.

— Dish Suggestion —
Compressed Strawberry and Tempura Elderflower.

Compressed Pear

INGREDIENTS

1 Soft pear

250ml Pear juice

50g Sugar

METHOD

1. Peel the pear and cut into quarters lengthways, remove the core and slice into 3mm long pieces.

2. Place the pear slices, sugar and pear juice in a bowl and toss together.

3. Now, put all the ingredients into a pouch and compress for the full duration of the vacuuming process.

4. After this place the pouch in the fridge until needed.

5. Leave the pear compressed for at least 1 hour until needed, allowing the pear juice to enter the slices giving it an intense flavour.

— Dish Suggestion —
Compressed Pear with Toasted Walnut and Brie.

Curing

Wet Cure

INGREDIENTS

2 Pints water

3 Bay leaves

10 Peppercorns

225g Salt

225g Sugar

1 tbsp/2g Thyme

1g Five Spice powder

METHOD

1. Infuse all ingredients in a pan, bring to the boil then turn down heat to a simmer.

2. Remove pan from heat once the sugar and salt is dissolved.

3. Leave to cool.

The cure can be stored in the fridge for up to one month and can be re-used for more than one recipe.

— Uses for Cures —

Whole Spatchcock Chicken.

Dry Cure

INGREDIENTS

110g Sea salt

85g Sugar

Zest of 2 lemons

Zest of 2 oranges

2 Bay leaves

8g Crushed juniper berries

4g Black pepper

5g Dill or Thyme — optional

METHOD

1. Blend all ingredients to a dry powder.

If vac-sealed the cure will keep for three months.

— Uses for Cures —

Pork Cheek, Pickled Apple, Sage and Onion Mash.

Whisky and Orange Cure

INGREDIENTS

100ml Whisky

100ml Water

60g Sugar

40g Salt

Zest of 3 oranges

2 Bay leaves

3 Sprigs thyme

1 tsp Crushed roasted coriander seeds

METHOD

1. Place all ingredients into a saucepan and bring to a simmer for 5 minutes – until all sugar and salt has dissolved.

2. Leave to cool for 15 to 20 minutes for full infusion.

The cure can be stored in the fridge for up to one month and can be re-used for more than one recipe.

— Uses for Cures —

Perfect Cure for Whisky Smoked Salmon.

Stout Cure

INGREDIENTS

1 pint Stout

1 pint Water

140g Salt

100g Sugar

15g All Spice berries – crushed

15g Juniper berries – crushed

1g Cloves

2 Star anise

4 Bay leaves

6 Sprigs thyme

Zest of 1 orange

METHOD

1. Infuse all ingredients in a pan. Simmer until salt and sugar has dissolved.

2. Leave to cool.

The cure can be stored in the fridge for up to one month and can be re-used for more than one recipe.

— Uses for Cures —

Beef Cheeks, Short Ribs or Rump of Beef.

Preserved Orange Cure

INGREDIENTS

5g Salt

100g Marmalade

Zest of 2 oranges

500ml Fresh orange juice

1g Chinese Five Spice

2 Sprigs of thyme

1 Bay leaf

6 Juniper berries — crushed

20ml Honey

6 Peppercorns — crushed

METHOD

1. Place the honey and orange juice in a pan and reduce to 100ml.

2. Add all of the other ingredients to the pan and bring to a simmer for 10 minutes.

3. Allow to cool.

The cure can be stored in the fridge for up to one month and can be used for more than one recipe.

— Uses for Cures —
Duck Breast, Pigeon, Pheasant and Duck Legs.

Barbeque Sauce

INGREDIENTS

500ml Tomato Sauce (ketchup)

500ml HP Sauce

50ml Cider vinegar

65ml Honey

30ml Maple syrup

1 tsp Dried chilli flakes

1 tsp Toasted fennel seeds

4 Cloves crushed garlic

200ml Stout

50ml Olive oil

75g Black peppercorns

20g Salt

Zest of 2 oranges

METHOD

1. Infuse all the ingredients together in a pan.

2. Pass through a sieve.

The cure can be stored in the fridge for up to one month and can be used for more than one recipe.

— Dish Suggestion —
Great for all BBQ meats.

Butters

With all flavoured butters you can cut off a piece and place in a pouch with any meat or fish — seal the pouch and place in your water bath.

Have a little experiment with how much butter to use and which flavours you like.

Basil, Tomato and Parmesan Butter

INGREDIENTS

200g Unsalted butter

4 tbsp Grated Parmesan

10 Basil leaves – finely chopped

1 tbsp Sun-dried tomatoes – chopped

¼ tsp Sea salt

METHOD

1. Leave butter out of the fridge to soften.

2. Beat butter in a bowl or machine.

3. Add all ingredients until incorporated.

4. Check for seasoning, roll up in parchment paper or cling film and set in the fridge.

5. Only a small amount of salt is required as Parmesan will add natural seasoning.

The butter can be stored in the fridge for two weeks, or in the freezer for up to three months.

— Uses for Butters —

Lamb dishes, Sous Vide Tomatoes, Chicken Legs.

Truffle Butter

INGREDIENTS

200g Unsalted butter

¼ tsp Salt

½ tsp Thyme

40g White or black truffle

METHOD

1. Soften butter as base recipe.

2. Grate truffle into the butter

3. Add Salt and thyme

4. Beat then roll in greaseproof paper.

The butter can be stored in the fridge for two weeks, or in the freezer for up to three months.

— Uses for Butters —

Chicken Breasts, Asparagus, Mushrooms or Veal.

Masala Butter

INGREDIENTS

200g Unsalted butter

100g Masala Marinade*

¼ tsp Salt

METHOD

1. Soften butter and add all ingredients.

2. Mould and preserve in fridge.

The butter can be stored in the fridge for two weeks, or in the freezer for up to three months.

See marinades.

— Uses for Butters —

Monkfish, Cod, Lobster, Pork, Lamb and Chicken Legs.

Barbeque Butter

INGREDIENTS

200g Unsalted butter

150g BBQ Sauce*

¼ tsp Salt

METHOD

1. Soften butter and add all ingredients.

2. Mould and preserve in fridge.

The butter can be stored in the fridge for two weeks, or in the freezer for up to three months.

See curing.

— Uses for Butters —

Pork Ribs, Beef Ribs, Chicken Leg and Monk Fish.

Spiced Butter

INGREDIENTS

200g Unsalted butter

¼ tsp Coriander seeds

¼ tsp Cumin seeds

¼ tsp Caraway seeds

¼ tsp Chilli Flakes (or chopped fresh)

¼ tsp Salt

¼ tsp Grated ginger

1 tsp Lemon juice

METHOD

1. Soften butter.

2. Toast off the seeds under a grill or a dry pan — when cool add to butter.

3. Grind down all of the spices in a pestle and mortar and add to butter.

4. Add the lemon juice, salt, ginger powder and beat together.

5. Mould and preserve in fridge.

The butter can be stored in the fridge for two weeks, or in the freezer for up to three months.

— Uses for Butters —

Chicken Legs, Pork Loin, Cod, Lobster and Monk Fish.

Lime and Vanilla Butter

INGREDIENTS

200g Unsalted butter

Juice and zest of 2 limes

Seeds of 3 vanilla pods (or vanilla extract to taste)

METHOD

1. Soften butter and add all ingredients.

2. Mould and preserve in fridge.

The butter can be stored in the fridge for two weeks, or in the freezer for up to three months.

— Uses for Butters —

Salmon Fillet, Poached Cod, Monk Fish and Lobster.

Herb Butter

INGREDIENTS

200g Unsalted butter

3 tbsp mixed chopped herbs

¼ tsp Salt

METHOD

1. Soften butter and add all ingredients.

2. Mould and preserve in fridge.

The butter can be stored in the fridge for two weeks, or in the freezer for up to three months.

Herbs to try –
Dill, Rosemary, Tarragon,
Parsley and Sage.

– Uses for Butters –
Great all round butter to use with anything.

Tamarind Butter Sauce

INGREDIENTS

125g Fresh tamarind

400ml Water

25ml Light soy sauce

½ Clove garlic

25g Fresh ginger – finely chopped

Juice of 2 limes

METHOD

1. Place all ingredients in a pan and bring to the boil.

2. Reduce by half.

3. Blend to a purée in a food processor and pass off through a fine sieve.

The butter can be stored in the fridge for two weeks, or in the freezer for up to three months.

– Uses for Butters –
Brilliant with parsnips.

Orange, Chestnut and Cranberry Butter

INGREDIENTS

200g Unsalted butter

50g Cranberry sauce

100g Chopped chestnuts

Juice and zest of 2 oranges

½ tsp Salt

2 tbsp Chopped sage

Pinch of Cinnamon

Pinch of Nutmeg

Pinch of Mixed Spice

METHOD

1. Soften butter and add all ingredients.

2. Mould and preserve in fridge.

The butter can be stored in the fridge for two weeks, or in the freezer for up to three months.

— Uses for Butters —
Turkey Breasts and Legs
— good holiday flavours.

Smoking

Oak Smoked Butter

A great way to introduce some interesting flavour when serving bread at a dinner party, or use to finish off a sauce for serving with fish.

INGREDIENTS

120g Unsalted good quality butter

PolyScience smoking gun

Oak smoked wood chips lightly soaked with water

METHOD

1. Place the butter in an air tight container or under a glass cloche.

2. Fill the container/cloche with smoke using the smoking gun.

3. Set aside for 10 minutes.

4. After 10 minutes – repeat the process again.

5. Repeat this process 6 to 8 times depending on the depth of smoke flavour required.

– Dish Suggestion –
Serve with Bread for a Dinner Party.

Applewood Smoked Brie with Honey

Smoking cheese is quite easy once you get the hang of it, have a little experiment with any cheese you like — you might be surprised!

INGREDIENTS

1 Small ripened Brie

2 tbsp Good quality honey

Pinch sea salt

PolyScience smoking gun

Smoked Applewood chips

METHOD

1. Bring the cheese up to room temperature as it will accept the smoke flavour better. Gently warm the honey and Salt in a small pan or microwave.

2. Brush the honey onto the Brie.

3. Place the Brie in an airtight container or cloche.

4. Fill the container/cloche with smoke using the smoking gun.

5. Set aside for 10 to 15 minutes.

6. After 10 minutes – repeat the process again.

7. Repeat this process 4 to 5 times depending on the depth of smoke flavour required.

The Cheese is ready to eat or refrigerate and keep up to 3 days.

– Dish Suggestion –

Applewood Smoked Brie with Ham and Watercress.

Smoked Cranberry Relish

Cranberries work really well with poultry and game, and smoking adds a whole other flavour dimension. Try this with turkey and Christmas dinner won't be the same.

INGREDIENTS

500g Cranberries

360g Brown sugar

Juice of ½ orange

½ Cinnamon stick

3 Star anise

½ Nutmeg – grated

150ml Port

2 Cloves

PolyScience smoking gun

Smoking chips

METHOD

1. Pre-heat your water bath to 95°C.

2. Place all ingredients in a large pouch and vac-seal.

3. Put the pouch into your water bath for 1 hour or until the cranberries start to pop open.

4. Remove the cranberries from the pouch and discard the cinnamon, star anise and cloves.

5. While the cranberries are still warm, place in an air tight container and smoke.

6. Stir the cranberries after each smoking to ensure the surface layer gets folded in.

7. For a fully flavoured relish we would recommend 5 or 6 hits of smoke.

1 hr
95°C
Eight
2
Easy
— Dish Suggestion —
Roast Pheasant, Smoked Cranberry Relish and Crispy Pancetta

Pickling

Pickling Liquor

INGREDIENTS

222ml Water

200ml White wine vinegar

1 Bay leaf

6 Peppercorns

6 Juniper berries — crushed

1 tsp Fennel seeds — toasted

Zest of ½ orange

6 Allspice berries

¼ Stick cinnamon

METHOD

1. Place all of the ingredients into a pan and simmer for 10 minutes.

2. Allow to cool.

3. Pass through a fine sieve.

Pickling liquor can be stored in the fridge for two months.

Sugar Stock

INGREDIENTS

400g Caster Sugar

400ml Water

METHOD

1. Pre-heat your water bath to 70°C.

2. Place sugar and water in a pouch and seal.

3. Put the pouch into your water bath for 1 hour.

4. Keep checking the water bath to make sure the water is covering the pouch.

5. Place the pouch in ice water until cold and keep in the fridge for up to three days, or serve immediately.

— Dish Suggestion —
Use in the Pickling Compression.

Marinades

Masala Marinade

INGREDIENTS

2 tbsp Olive oil

1 Medium onion – sliced

3 Garlic cloves – crushed

2 Lemongrass sticks – sliced

25g Ginger – sliced

1 Red chilli – sliced

5g Coriander seeds – roasted

5g Cumin seeds – roasted

5g Pepper corns – roasted

5g Fennel seeds – roasted

5g Curry powder – roasted

Zest of ½ orange

Zest of 2 limes

Zest of 1 lemon

500ml Tomato passata

METHOD

1. Gently fry the onions, garlic, lemongrass, ginger and chilli until softened.

2. Add Roasted spices and zests.

3. Add passata and cook for 20 minutes until soft.

4. Blend in a food processor to make the marinade.

Marinade can be stored in the fridge for one month.

– Dish Suggestion –

Use with Monkfish, Chicken, Lamb, Pork or even Potatoes.

Salmon, Cod, Halibut,
Mackerel, Monkfish,
Skate, Seafood Burger,
Pollock, Tuna, Sea Bass,
Lobster and Langoustines.

Fish

To cook a fillet of fish or a portioned skate wing precisely, is a skill in itself. Too little and it's raw and could be dangerous to consume or too much and it becomes dry and flavourless due to all the moisture being lost.

This is where sous vide cooking comes into its own. By following the times and temperatures in this book, you will be able to achieve perfect cooking with no loss of flavour. The proteins of fish will contract slower so as not to push out or lose any natural moisture, or flavour. Where as pan frying or grilling makes the proteins contract quicker forcing moisture out of the cell walls producing a tougher texture and dry mouth feel.

Salmon *smoked*

01

The delicate texture of smoked salmon is ramped up when using a water bath. The melt in your mouth flavours will make this a favourite at any dinner party.

INGREDIENTS

8 Salmon portions – skinned and cleaned, each 75-100g

PolyScience smoking gun

Wet Cure, see ***curing***

STAGE 1

1. Firstly you'll need to cure your salmon for 6 hours. This will make the flesh lovely and moist. Follow the ***wet cure*** instructions in the ***curing*** section.

STAGE 2

2. Pre-heat your water bath to 40°C.

3. Rinse your salmon to remove the wet cure and cold smoke using a PolyScience smoking gun – you will need to apply 6 hits of smoke.

4. Place your salmon portions into pouches and vac-seal.

Depending on the size of your pouches, you might want to seal them individually or in pairs.

5. Now, place the freshly sealed pouches into your water bath for between 45 minutes and 1 hour.

6. Keep checking the water bath to make sure the water is covering the pouches.

7. A couple of minutes before the time is up, prepare some ice water ready to place the pouches in.

8. When the time is up, 'refresh' the pouches immediately in the ice water, remove the salmon and serve.

Chef's Tip –
Instead of using a wet cure try covering the salmon with salt & sugar (60g of each) for 30 minutes then rinse.

1 hr
40°C
Eight
3
Med
— Dish Suggestion —
Smoked Organic Salmon,
Pickled Apple, Wild Dill
and Bagel Crisps.

Salmon with Whisky and Orange

02

The combination of whisky, orange and salmon really is worth trying, even if you don't like whisky. The flavours take the salmon to another level and transform the popular fish.

INGREDIENTS

6 Salmon portions, each 100g

150ml Whisky

50g Sugar

½ Vanilla pod

10g Salt

Zest of 1 orange

20 Crushed juniper berries

2 tbsp Chopped dill

100ml White wine

METHOD

1. Pre-heat your water bath to 50°C.

2. Place all your ingredients with the exception of the salmon into a pan, bring to the boil and reduce by half. Then it's hands off until it's cool.

3. Place your salmon portions into pouches, pour in the whisky reduction and vac-seal. If you have an external vacuum sealer either vacuum seal using a zip lock bag instead or freeze the reduction in an ice cube tray and add to the bag before vacuum sealing with your external vacuum sealer.

Depending on the size of your pouches, you might want to seal them individually or in pairs.

4. Now, place the sealed pouches into your water bath for between 45 minutes.

5. Keep checking the water bath to make sure the water is covering the pouches.

6. When the time is up, the delicious smelling salmon is ready to serve.

Chef's Tip —
Any form of marinade goes well with Salmon. Try the masala one in the 'marinades' section for a spicy finish.

45 mins
50°C
Six
2
Easy
— Dish Suggestion —
Whisky and Vanilla cured Salmon with a simple Herb Salad.

03

Cured Cod

We've all eaten cod, but curing it before cooking improves flavour and texture. This helps to elevate the cod into something that will surprise and delight.

INGREDIENTS

4 Cod portions, each 150g

CURE INGREDIENTS

150g Sea salt

150g Sugar

8 Peppercorns

30g Chopped dill

Zest of 2 lemons

STAGE 1

1. Firstly you'll need to blend the ***cure ingredients*** ready to cover your cod.

2. Place your cod portions in a tray and sprinkle with the blended mixture.

3. Now, put the tray in the fridge for 6 hours, this will firm up the flesh before cooking.

STAGE 2

4. After 6 hours, thoroughly rinse the cod in cold running water.

5. Pre-heat your water bath to 52°C.

6. Place the cod portions into pouches and vac-seal.

Depending on the size of your pouches, you might want to seal them individually or in pairs.

7. Pop the sealed pouches of cod into your water bath for 50 minutes.

8. Keep checking the water bath to make sure the water is covering the pouches.

9. Remove the beautifully cured cod from the pouches and serve.

Chef's Tip —
The cod can be smoked prior to cooking, after the curing.

50 mins
52°C
Four
3
Med
– Dish Suggestion –
Slow Cooked Cured Cod, Roasted Pumpkin and Wild Mushrooms.

04

Halibut Confit

A great alternative to cod or haddock, halibut is firmer in texture and takes on flavours really well. It adds a 'posh' feeling to that traditional fish supper.

INGREDIENTS

2 Halibut portions, each 150g — skin off

4 fl oz Olive oil

4 Fennel tops — or dill Sprigs

Salt

Zest of ½ lemon

Dill pollen (optional)

METHOD

1. Pre-heat your water bath to 55°C.

2. Remove any 'blood line' from the underside of the halibut or ask your fishmonger to do this for you.

3. Season the halibut on both sides and sprinkle with the dill pollen.

4. Place the halibut into pouches, along with the olive oil, dill sprigs and lemon zest, vac-seal.

Depending on the size of your pouches, you might want to seal them individually.

5. Now, put the sealed pouches of halibut into your water bath for 15 minutes.

6. Keep checking the water bath to make sure the water is covering the pouches.

7. Check the halibut after 12 minutes, if you like a softer texture, then remove now and let the halibut rest.

If you prefer a firmer texture, leave the halibut for 18 minutes and then check.

8. Remove the halibut from the pouch, pat dry with kitchen towel and serve immediately.

The halibut portions can be finished in a hot pan to give a roasted flavour.

Chef's Tip —
Try replacing the oil with milk to keep the halibut white.

15 mins
55°C
Four
3
Med
— Dish Suggestion —
Confit of Halibut with Charred Leeks and Fennel.

05

Smoked Mackerel

Mackerel, being an oily fish, benefits from being smoked. But when it's charred too, the elevated flavour and texture create a dish to die for.

INGREDIENTS

2 Mackerel fillets

1 Sous vide beetroot portion — see ***vegetable*** section

50g Fresh horseradish — grated

100g Horseradish relish

200g Good quality soft cheese

100g Cream — semi-whipped

PolyScience smoking gun

Smoking chips

STAGE 1

1. Place your mackerel fillets in an airtight container or under a glass cloche.

2. Smoke with the gun and leave to stand for 5 minutes.

3. Repeat this process between 4 and 6 times depending on the desired intensity of flavour.

STAGE 2

4. Roast the beetroot by following the ***beetroot*** instructions in the ***vegetable*** section.

5. Blend the soft cheese, horseradish relish and grated horseradish together and then fold in the lovely cream.

6. Place the resulting mousse in a piping bag and set aside ready for serving.

7. Char the mackerel on the skin side with a blow torch or under a hot grill.

8. Finish the cooking of the mackerel off under the grill.

9. Pipe the horseradish mousse on to a plate together with the beetroot and mackerel — prepare yourself for a tasty lunch or snack.

Chef's Tip —
The smoking can be done a couple of days in advance and charred just before serving.

35 mins
7 times
Two
4
Med
— Dish Suggestion —
Smoked Mackerel, Roasted Beetroot and Horseradish Mousse.

06

Masala Monkfish

Monkfish has a wonderful meaty texture that works really well with the spicy masala flavours. The orange-tinged outside and soft white flesh look amazing on the plate.

INGREDIENTS

6 Monkfish portions, each 150g — cleaned

Masala Butter, see ***butters***

STAGE 1

1. Firstly you'll need to make your masala butter. Follow the ***masala butter*** instructions in the ***butters*** section.

STAGE 2

2. Pre-heat your water bath to 48°C.

3. Brush the monkfish all over with masala butter.

4. Place your monkfish portions into pouches and vac-seal.

Depending on the size of your pouches, you might want to seal them individually or in pairs.

5. Then, place the sealed pouches into your water bath for between 16 and 18 minutes.

6. Keep checking the water bath to make sure the water is covering the pouches.

7. Remove the monkfish from the pouches, pat dry with kitchen towel, and quickly pan fry for extra colour.

Chef's Tip —
Dust the fish with any dry powder — curry powder, will dill pollen or ras-el-hanout — each give a delightful flavour.

18 mins
48°C
Six
3
Med
— Dish Suggestion —
Masala Roasted Monkfish, Soy Roasted Lettuce and Butternut Squash.

07

Rolled Lime and Vanilla Skate

Lime and vanilla are the perfect flavours for this delicate fish, together with the lemongrass you'll be in Asian-flavour heaven.

INGREDIENTS

2 Medium skate wings, each 300–400g

3 Sticks Lemongrass

100ml Olive oil

Salt

Pepper

Lime and Vanilla Butter, see ***butters***

STAGE 1

1. Firstly you'll need to make your lime and lemon butter. Follow the instructions in the ***butters*** section.

STAGE 2

2. Pre-heat your water bath to 56°C.

3. Using a flexible but sharp knife, remove the meat from the skate wing bone – or you can ask your fishmonger to do this.

4. Now, pull out some cling film and lay the flesh side by side. Spread the beautiful lime and vanilla butter all over the flesh.

5. Roll the skate into a cylinder shape using the cling film and set in the fridge for 2 hours.

STAGE 3

6. While you're waiting, blend the lemongrass and salt with the olive oil and place in a pouch ready for the fish.

7. Take the fish from the fridge – carefully removing the cling film – pop into the pouch and vac-seal.

8. Place the sealed pouches into your water bath for 45 minutes.

9. Keep checking the water bath to make sure the water is covering the pouches.

10. Once ready, serve immediately.

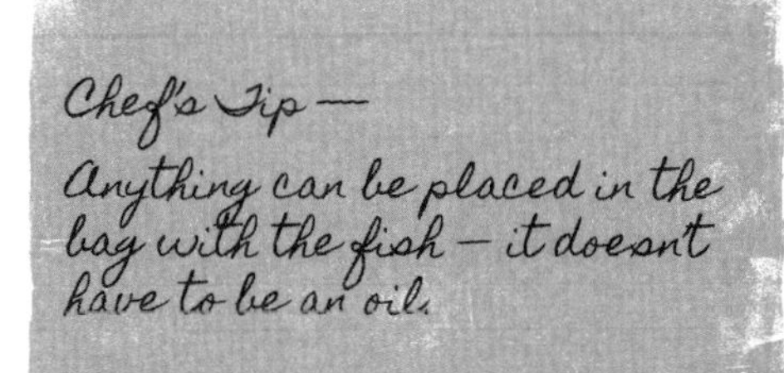

45 mins
56°C
Two
5
Hard
— Dish Suggestion —
Lime Confit Skate wing with Caper Butter and Spinach.

08

Seafood Burger

There's something all together more decadent with this mouth-watering burger. You'll wonder why you've stuck with beef all this time.

INGREDIENTS

50g Smoked haddock

50g Salmon

50g Cod

50g Lobster

1 Egg – beaten

¼ tsp Salt

½ tsp Chopped dill

Juice of ½ lemon

Zest of ½ lemon

METHOD

1. Pre-heat your water bath to 58°C, or 62°C for a firmer finish.

2. Cut the fish into small, fine pieces – but you still want chunks to hold the burger together.

3. Place the fish in a bowl with the other ingredients and mix.

4. Use a 3½ inch cutter to create the perfect burger shape, pressing the mix down so it's nice and compact.

5. Rub the top and bottom of the burger with oil, place in a pouch and vac-seal.

Depending on the size of your pouches, you might want to seal them individually or in pairs.

6. For a medium burger pop the pouches in your water bath at 58°C for 40 minutes.

Or for a firmer, more well done burger try 62°C for 40 minutes.

7. Keep checking the water bath to make sure the water is covering the pouches.

8. Remove the burgers and pat dry with kitchen towel. Season and colour in a hot pan until the outside is crisp.

Chef's Tip —
Try using a flavoured butter.

40 mins
58°C
Two
4
Med
— Dish Suggestion —
Serve in a Sesame Seed Ciabatta Roll with Cucumber and Spinach.

Pollock

09

It's lovely to have a fish available like pollock, it's a little underrated but has great texture and big flavour lending itself to compliment mussels without becoming second fiddle.

INGREDIENTS

2 Pollock portions
– 2cm thick from flat fillet at 150g

500g Mussels

50ml Crème fraîche

30g Tomato – diced

50g Broad beans

½ tsp Sea salt

300ml White wine

2 tbsp Parsley – chopped

Juice of 1 lemon

STAGE 1

1. Pre-heat your water bath to 60°C.

2. Place a deep, tall pan on the stove and allow to get hot.

3. Put the mussels in the hot pan along with the white wine and parsley – cover with the lid immediately.

4. Allow the mussels to open before removing and straining off – keep the liquor to one side.

STAGE 2

5. Season the pollock on both sides with the salt and gently rub with oil to prevent any sticking.

6. Put the pollock in a pouch, along with the mussel liquor, and vac-seal. If you have an external vacuum sealer vacuum sealer either use a zip bag lock bag to create a vacuum instead or leave the mussel liquor out of the pouch and use your vacuum sealer. Save the mussel liquor for step 11.

7. Place the pouch in your water bath for 40 minutes.

8. Keep checking the water bath to make sure the water is covering the pouch.

9. Remove the pollock and carefully peel off the skin.

10. Season with some more salt and lemon juice before serving.

11. Return the cooking juices from the pouch to a pan and bring to the boil.

12. Gently fold in the crème fraîche and finally add the diced tomato and broad beans.

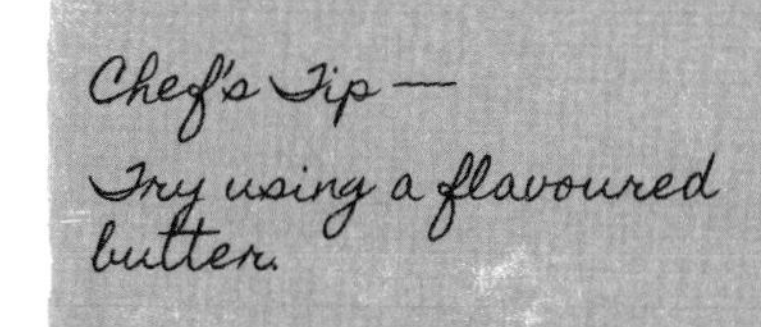

40 mins
60°C
Two
3
Med
— Dish Suggestion —
Pollock poached with Mussels, Broad Beans and Tomato.

10

Confit Tuna Belly

We're using the belly from the tuna as it's the tastiest part of the fish. It lends itself to confit really well as it has a lot of natural flavour and fat. Perfect with toast.

INGREDIENTS

1kg Tuna belly

500ml Virgin olive oil

200g Dried oregano

Zest of 2 limes

Zest of 2 oranges

Dry Cure, see ***curing***

STAGE 1

1. Ask your fishmonger to remove any excess sinew from the belly or you can have a go yourself if you prefer.

2. Cover the belly on all sides with the ***dry cure*** mixture and leave for 3 hours in the fridge covered with cling film.

3. After the 3 hours, wash the tuna under cold running water and pat dry with kitchen towel.

STAGE 2

4. Pre-heat your water bath to 68°C.

5. Now, put the tuna in a large pouch, along with the olive oil, oregano, lime zest and orange zest, vac-seal.

6. Place the pouch in your water bath for 2 hours.

8. Keep checking the water bath to make sure the water is covering the pouch.

9. Remove the tuna and again pat dry with kitchen towel. Serve immediately.

*Chef's Tip —
The simplicity of this dish can be altered by changing the herb, used to create a different dynamic.*

2 hrs
68°C
Four
2
Easy
– Dish Suggestion –
Confit Belly of Tuna with Oregano and Citrus

11

Wild Sea Bass

Wild Sea bass is much firmer and thicker than its cousin the farmed sea bass. Because of this, the sous vide method of cooking works really well and creates an almost steak-like texture.

INGREDIENTS

2 Wild sea bass portion, each 140g — thick cut, descaled and pinboned

¼ tsp Salt

Wild dill pollen — finely chopped dill fonds

1 tsp Oil

METHOD

1. Pre-heat your water bath to 50°C.

2. Ensure all the scales and pinbones are removed from the fish.

3. Place skin side down and season the flesh with the salt and sprinkle with the dill pollen.

4. Gently rub the skin and flesh with a little oil, place in a pouch and vac-seal.

5. Place the pouch in your water bath for 30 minutes.

6. Keep checking the water bath to make sure the water is covering the pouch.

7. Remove the sea bass and pat dry with kitchen towel.

8. Crisp the skin in a pan and serve immediately, delicious and hot.

Chef's Tip —
You can use normal seabass but at a lower temperature and time — you will loose some texture and flavour.

30 mins
50°C
Two
2
Easy
– Dish Suggestion –
Wild Sea Bass
with Asparagus and
Charred Lemon.

12

Lobster

An expensive ingredient for professionals and amateurs alike, so the cooking needs to be exact. Butter packing the lobster infuses herb and citrus flavours into the already sweet, sweet flesh.

INGREDIENTS

1 Lobster broken down into 2 claws and 1 tail, weighing 2lb

¼ Sea salt

Zest of 1 lemon

200g Herb Butter, see ***butters***

METHOD

1. Pre-heat your water bath to 54°C.

2. Put a pan of water on to boil and add salt to taste.

3. When the water is boiling place the lobster claws in for 3 minutes, then place in ice water.

4. Allow the pan to return to a boil.

5. Cook the lobster tail for 1½ minutes in the boiling water, then place in ice water.

6. Now, remove the meat from inside the tail and claws popping in a pouch, along with the ***herb butter,*** lemon zest and sea salt, vac-seal.

7. Place the sealed pouch into your water bath for 35 minutes.

8. Keep checking the water bath to make sure the water is covering the pouch.

9. Gently remove the lobster from the pouch and serve immediately.

Or, portion the tail in two lengthways and brown off in a hot pan to add a crispy caramelised flavour.

Chef's Tip —
Use a spiced butter and spread it all over the lobster tail.

3
35 mins
54°C
Two
Med
— Dish Suggestion —
Herb Butter Poached Lobster with Watermelon

13

Langoustines

These are delicious little morsels of sweetness, helped along with citrus and herb flavours, and so easy to prepare and cook. A huge percentage are exported to Europe, get hold of them if you can.

INGREDIENTS

10 Large langoustines

½ Rosemary sprig
– de-stemed and chopped finely

1 strip of lemon zest

1 strip of lime zest

200ml Light olive oil

¼ tsp Sea salt

METHOD

1. Pre-heat your water bath to 54°C.

2. Put a pan of water on to boil and add salt to taste.

3. Pull the heads off the langoustines by holding the head in one hand, and the tail in the other, twisting in opposite directions.

4. Add the langoustines to the pan for 10 seconds, then place in ice water.

5. Remove the langoustine tails from the ice water when cold and pinch together in your fingers until the shell cracks. Then gently remove the shell and intestine tract from the tail meat.

6. Now, put in a pouch, along with the remaining ingredients, and vac-seal.

7. Place the sealed pouch into your water bath for 15 minutes.

8. Keep checking the water bath to make sure the water is covering the pouch.

9. Remove the langoustines from the pouch and pat dry with kitchen towel.

10. Colour off in a hot pan and serve immediately.

Chef's Tip —
Any herb can be used to create an infusion of flavour.

15 mins
54°C
Two
4
Med
— Dish Suggestion —
Rosemary and Citrus Langoustines.

Pork, Chicken, Turkey,
Pheasant, Pigeon, Duck,
Beef, Lamb and Venison.

Meat

Achieving the perfect cooking of a steak or larger piece of meat can be a tough job even for the professional chef. This section will guide you through accurate processes achieving amazing flavours and textures. Flavour lock in is important for all the recipes in this book, and the process of sous vide cookery can create perfection time and time again.

You'll quickly gain confidence to go on and experiment with other flavours, accomplishing quality and consistency.

Pork Belly

14

Everyone loves crackling, and pork belly is the cut you want to make a great impression. You can even sous vide this in advance and finish off in a hot pan, filling the kitchen with amazing smells and setting mouths watering.

INGREDIENTS

2kg Pork belly

Wet Cure, see ***curing***

STAGE 1

1. Firstly you'll need to cure your pork belly for 24 hours. This will make the meat so tasty you'll wonder why you don't do it all the time.

Just follow the ***wet cure*** instructions in the ***curing*** section.

STAGE 2

2. Pre-heat your water bath to 62°C for a 72 hour cooking time, or 64°C for a 48 hour cooking time.

3. Remove your pork belly from the wet cure and rinse under cold running water.

4. Now, cut the pork belly into nice portions, giving yourself a bigger piece!

5. Place the portions into pouches and vac-seal.

6. Now, put the pouches into your water bath for the time that's right for you. Either 72 hours at 62°C, or 48 hours at 64°C.

7. Keep checking the water bath to make sure the water is covering the pouches.

8. Once the pork belly is cooked, remove from the pouches and place on a baking tray. Then, place another baking tray on top of the pork belly portions, weighing it down slightly and refrigerate.

This will give you perfectly straight portions ready for finishing in a hot pan.

9. Remove the top skin from the belly and pan fry, giving a butter like texture inside and a roasted exterior.

Chef's Tip —
Instead of curing — place the Pork Belly in pouches and add Cider before sealing.

72 hrs
62°C
Six
5
Hard
– Dish Suggestion –
Pork Belly with Toffee Apple and Sage.

15

Smoked Pork Belly

When cooking pork belly using the Sous Vide method, all the natural fats melt slowly and baste the meat underneath. So when an Applewood Smoke is added before cooking, the smoke will penetrate through all of the meat during it's cooking time too.

INGREDIENTS

2kg Pork belly — bone out

PolyScience smoking gun

Applewood smoking chips

STAGE 1

1. Pre-heat your water bath to 62°C for a 72 hour cooking time, or 64°C for a 48 hour cooking time.

2. Ask your butcher to remove the bones to make it easier to cook your Pork belly.

3. Place the pork belly in to a deep tray with high sides that rise above the meat — cover with cling film tightly.

4. Make a small hole in the cling film and insert the smoking tube. Cover the meat in the Applewood smoke and cover the hole.

Repeat this process 10 times for a deep, smoky flavour.

STAGE 2

5. Place your pork belly into a pouch and vac-seal. Then, pop the pouch into your water bath for the time that's right for you.

6. Keep checking the water bath to make sure the water is covering the pouch.

7. Once the pork belly is cooked, place the pouch in ice water for 5 minutes.

8. Now, remove the pork belly from the pouch and place on a baking tray. Pop another baking tray on top of the pork, weighing it down slightly. Put the tray in your fridge for around 1 hour.

9. Cut the pork belly into portions and remove the skin.

You can smoke it again to add more smokiness if desired at this stage.

10. Crisp the pork belly in a hot pan fat side first then all over.

Chef's Tip —
To add another flavour to the pork why not brush with maple syrup.

72 hrs
62°C
Six
5
Hard
— Dish Suggestion —
Smoked Pork Belly with
Sweetcorn and Pear.

16

Pork Cheeks

Soft enough for no knife, succulent and a fairly cheap off-cut of pork, these delicious cheeks are worth the hunt at your butchers. They will fast become part of your dinner menu.

INGREDIENTS

6 Pork cheeks – sinew removed

150ml Cider

150ml Pork stock

1 Sage leaf

WET CURE INGREDIENTS

2 Pints water

3 Bay leaves

10 Peppercorns

225g Salt

225g Sugar

1 tbsp/2g Thyme

1g Five Spice powder

STAGE 1

1. Infuse all wet cure ingredients in a pan, bring to the boil then turn down heat to a simmer.

2. Remove the pan from heat once the sugar and salt have dissolved. Leave to cool.

3. Cover the pork cheeks in the liquid and pop in the fridge for 12 hours.

4. Remove the pork cheeks and rinse under cold running water for 10 minutes.

STAGE 2

5. Pre-heat your water bath to 85°C.

6. Pan fry the pork cheeks to get an even caramelisation and leave to cool.

7. Once cooled, place your pork cheeks into a pouch, together with the cider, pork stock and sage leaf and vac-seal. If using an external vacuum sealer create a vacuum using a zip lock bag instead.

8. Keep checking the water bath to make sure the water is covering the pouch.

9. After 12 hours, remove the pork cheeks from the pouch and reserve the liquor from the bag for a sauce.

The pork cheeks can stay in the fridge for 3 to 5 days – regenerate at 85°C for 25 minutes when needed.

Chef's Tip —
Try braising the pork cheeks in a sweet and sour sauce.

12 hrs
85°C
Two
4
Med
— Dish Suggestion —
Slow Cooked Ox Cheeks, Butter Poached Carrots and Mash.

17

Pork Fillet

Also known as the tenderloin, this is the eye fillet that comes from within the pork loin. It's lean, very tender and works amazingly with sweet, sticky flavours.

INGREDIENTS

4 Pork fillets, each 180g – fully trimmed

2 tbsp Maple syrup

Zest of ½ orange

2 tbsp Olive oil

Pinch Chinese Five Spice

Pinch salt

STAGE 1

1. Pre-heat your water bath to 62°C for a medium pork fillet.

2. In a bowl, add the syrup, zest, oil and Five Spice. Mix in the pork fillets and leave to marinate for 1 hour.

STAGE 2

3. When the hour is up, individually wrap each fillet in cling film to help keep uniformity of shape.

4. Place the pork into a pouch and vac-seal.

Depending on the size of your pouches, you might want to seal them individually or in pairs.

5. Now, put the pouches into your water bath for 45 minutes.

6. Keep checking the water bath to make sure the water is covering the pouch.

7. Place a little oil in a frying pan and sear the finished fillets for a delicious roast caramelised flavour.

Be a little careful when caramelising due to the sugar content in maple syrup.

8. Season with salt and serve.

To regenerate from cold place the pouch in the water bath at 62°C for 20 minutes and finish in a hot pan.

Chef's Tip — Try lightly smoking the pork fillet before marinating.

45 mins
62°C
Four
4
Med
— Dish Suggestion —
Maple Cured Pork Fillet, Spiced Butternut Squash, Crackling and Sage.

18

Baby Back Pork Ribs

Aromatic, sticky, succulent finger food ideal for lazy, sunny BBQs... to be honest they're great any time finished in the oven!

INGREDIENTS

2 Baby Back Pork Ribs

Wet Cure, see ***curing***

BBQ Sauce, see ***marinades***

STAGE 1

1. Split your baby back ribs into three pieces and place in the ***wet cure*** for 12 hours.

Just follow the ***wet cure*** instructions in the ***curing*** section.

STAGE 2

2. Pre-heat your water bath to 64°C.

3. Remove the ribs from the cure and rinse under cold running water for 10 minutes. Then pat dry with kitchen towel.

4. Place the ribs into a pouch and pour over the BBQ sauce, then vac-seal.

Depending on the size of your pouches, you might want to seal the pieces individually.

5. Now, put the pouches into your water bath for 48 hours.

6. Keep checking the water bath to make sure the water is covering the pouch.

7. Remove the sticky ribs and serve immediately or place the pouches in ice water and then leave in the fridge.

8. Grill or roast the ribs to finish them off ready for some finger-licking fun!

To regenerate from cold brush a little more BBQ sauce on the ribs and grill or roast for 5 minutes until hot.

Chef's Tip —
A dry spice rub is perfect to add a little zing to ribs.

2
48 hrs
64°C
Two
Easy
– Dish Suggestion –
BBQ Ribs, House Slaw,
Smoked Sweetcorn

Chinese Five Spice Pork Chops

19

The Five Spice adds a mouth-watering fragrancy to the chops that makes them so moorish. That coupled with crisp fat will leave you wanting more.

INGREDIENTS

4 Pork chops, each 280g

2 Sticks lemongrass

20g Chinese Five Spice

20g Fresh coriander

5g Dried chilli flakes

½ tsp Salt

½ tsp Crushed peppercorns

100ml Olive oil

1 Garlic clove

METHOD

1. Pre-heat your water bath to 64°C.

2. Mix all the ingredients, except the pork chops, in a small blender or pestle and mortar to make a wet marinade.

3. Rub the marinade generously on the pork chops.

4. Now, place the chops into a pouch and vac-seal.

Depending on the size of your pouches, you might want to seal the chops individually or in pairs.

5. Now, put the pouches into your water bath for 40 minutes.

6. Keep checking the water bath to make sure the water is covering the pouch.

7. Finish straight onto a char-grill or griddle pan. You can place the pouches in ice water and then leave in the fridge for later if you need.

To regenerate from cold place the pouch in the water bath at 62°C for 20 minutes and finish on a char-grill or in a griddle pan.

Chef's Tip —
Use masala butter or maple glaze.

40 mins
64°C
Four
2
Easy
— Dish Suggestion —
Chinese Five Spice Pork, Tamarind Roasted Parsnip and Smoked Apple.

20

Festive Ham

Once you've tried this you won't just want 'festive ham' at Christmas time, you'll want it any time. Tender melt in your mouth ham, crisp and sticky fat... what are you waiting for?

INGREDIENTS

1 Piece of Horse Shoe Gammon, weighing 2½–3kg

80g Dijon mustard

65g Maple syrup

65g Honey

Peel of 2 oranges

2 tsp Mixed spice

6 Bay leaves

6 Star anise

200ml Cola

20 Juniper berries

1 tsp Chopped thyme

100ml Ginger syrup — from stem ginger

6 Cloves

STAGE 1

1. Pre-heat your water bath to 65°C.

2. Place all the ingredients, except the gammon, in a saucepan and simmer gently for 15 minutes. Set aside to cool.

3. When completely cold, put the liquor in a pouch, along with the gammon, and vac-seal.

4. Now, put the pouch into your water bath for 12 hours.

5. Keep checking the water bath to make sure the water is covering the pouch.

STAGE 2

6. Just before the gammon is ready, pre-heat your oven to 200°C.

7. When the cooking time is up, remove the gammon from it's pouch and roast in the oven for 10 minutes for lovely, crispy fat.

The gammon can be prepared 2 days in advance and chilled in ice water. To regenerate place the pouch in the water bath at 65°C for 3 hours and then roast to crisp the fat.

Chef's Tip —
Rub the ham with cranberry and marmalade with some added sage.

12 hrs
65°C
Eight
2
Easy
— Dish Suggestion —
Make your festive ham the star and keep it simple with a selection of pickles and crusty bread.

21

Whole Spatchcock Chicken

The technique of 'spatchcocking' the chicken exposes more of the skin, which in turn helps to make the meat lovely and juicy. Say goodbye to dry chicken!

INGREDIENTS

1–1½kg Chicken

1 Chicken stock cube

1 tsp Thyme

50ml Olive oil

Wet Cure, see ***curing***

STAGE 1

1. Using 'butchers scissors' – cut out the back bone and sternum of the chicken.

2. Firmly press down on the chicken breasts to flatten, also known as 'butterflying'.

3. Place the chicken in the ***wet cure*** and keep in the fridge for 24 hours.

STAGE 2

4. Pre-heat your water bath to 68°C.

5. Remove the chicken from cure and rinse under cold running water for 10 minutes. Then pat dry with kitchen towel.

6. Brush the chicken with 50ml olive oil and crumble the stock cube over the chicken along with the thyme.

7. Put the chicken into a pouch and vac-seal.

8. Now, put the pouch into your water bath for 4 hours.

9. Keep checking the water bath to make sure the water is covering the pouch.

10. After the 4 hours, remove the chicken from it's pouch and pat dry with kitchen towel.

11. Roast in an oven or frying pan until the skin is lovely and crisp.

To regenerated from cold place the pouch in the water bath at 68°C water for 40 minutes and finish in the oven.

Chef's Tip —
Smoke the chicken before you vac-seal and cook at the same temperature & time.

4 hrs
68°C
Four
5
Hard
— Dish Suggestion —
Roasted Chicken with
Truffle Poached Leeks.

22

Coconut Spiced Chicken

We all like a good curry, and chicken really lends itself to masala flavouring. Try this takeaway-beater for an indulgent night in.

STAGE 1 INGREDIENTS

6 Chicken thighs

6 Chicken drumsticks

Dry Cure, see ***curing***

STAGE 2 INGREDIENTS

200ml Coconut Milk

100ml Yoghurt

30g Coriander — chopped

60 ml Masala Marinade, see ***marinades***

STAGE 1

1. Firstly sprinkle the thighs and drumsticks with the ***dry cure*** and marinade in the fridge for 2 hours.

2. After the 2 hours rinse under cold running water and pat dry with kitchen towel.

STAGE 2

3. Pre-heat your water bath to 68°C.

4. Mix the coconut milk and yoghurt together. Then in a hot pan seal the chicken thighs and drumsticks.

5. Put the chicken into a pouch, add the ***masala marinade,*** chopped coriander and vac-seal.

6. Now, put the pouch into your water bath for 4 hours 30 minutes.

7. Keep checking the water bath to make sure the water is covering the pouch.

8. When the time is up warm through the coconut and yoghurt mix along with the juices and marinade from the pouch to create a tasty sauce, add the chicken just before you serve.

You can place the pouch in ice water and then leave in the fridge for up to three days.

To regenerate from cold place the pouch in your water bath for 45 minutes at 75°C, or place in a hot oven.

Chef's Tip —
Use roasted mushrooms, red wine and chicken stock to create a nice red wine chicken.

4½ hrs
68°C
Four
2
Easy
— Dish Suggestion —
Coconut Spiced Chicken
with Steamed Rice.

23

Chicken Supreme

Succulent and moist chicken is the stuff of dreams, and with sous vide cooking you also get a softer texture taking the once familiar to new levels.

INGREDIENTS

4 Chicken Supremes, each 220g

½ tsp Sea salt

50 ml Olive oil

1 Chicken stock cube

METHOD

1. Pre-heat your water bath to 64°C.

2. Trim all sinew from the chicken supreme leaving the skin on.

3. Brush the chicken supremes with the olive oil and season with sea salt, then crumble the stock cube over the skin.

4. Put the chicken into a pouch and vac-seal.

Depending on the size of your pouches, you might want to seal the chicken individually.

5. Now, put the pouches into your water bath for 45 minutes.

6. Keep checking the water bath to make sure the water is covering the pouch.

7. When the time is up, remove from the pouch and pat dry with kitchen towel.

8. Colour the skin of the chicken in a hot pan and you're ready to serve.

You can place the pouches in ice water and then leave in the fridge for up to three days.

To regenerate from cold place the pouches in your water bath for 20 minutes at 64°C and finish by sealing in a hot pan to crisp the skin and give a roasted flavour.

Chef's Tip —
Try 2 tablespoons of truffle butter or any herb butter in the pouch.

45 mins
64°C
Four
2
Easy
— Dish Suggestion —
Chicken Supreme, charred Asparagus and crispy Chicken Skin.

Tandoori Chicken

24

Traditionally chicken tandoori is marinaded for 4 to 6 hours after piercing holes in the chicken all over. We will be using a chicken breast covered in marinade,that takes less time due to it being vacuum sealed.

INGREDIENTS

2 Chicken supremes — skin on

200ml Yoghurt

2 tsp Ginger — crushed finely

2 tsp Garlic — crushed finely

½ tsp Chilli powder

1 tsp Coriander seeds — ground and toasted

¼ tsp Garam Masala — ground

¼ tsp Cinnamon — ground

2 tsp Lemon juice

1 tbsp Flour

¼ tsp Orange food colour

½ tsp Fenugreek powder

1 tbsp Vegetable oil

Pinch of salt

60g Melted butter

STAGE 1

1. Pre-heat your water bath to 64°C.

2. Toast off the coriander seeds and grind up with a pestle and mortar.

3. Add all the ingredients, apart from the chicken, in a bowl and combine with a whisk to a smooth marinade.

4. Season the chicken on both sides and place into a pouch adding the marinade, and vac-seal.

Depending on the size of your pouches, you might want to seal the chicken individually.

5. Leave the pouches in the fridge for between 1 and 2 hours.

STAGE 2

6. Now, put the pouches into your water bath for 1 hour.

7. Keep checking the water bath to make sure the water is covering the pouches.

8. When the time is up remove the chicken from the pouches and colour, skin side down, in a hot pan whilst the marinade caramelises.

9. Add the contents of the bag to create a lovely sauce. A small amount of water may be needed to bring the sauce together.

Chef's Tip —
The chicken could be simply poached in a masala butter recipe.

1 hr
64°C
Two
3
Med
— Dish Suggestion —
Tandoori Chicken,
Braised Red Lentils and
Coriander Chutney.

25

Confit Chicken Wings

Cooking the chicken wings in duck fat makes them wonderfully moist and tender, this and the crispy skin beats anything that comes in a bucket.

INGREDIENTS

1kg Chicken wings

500ml Duck fat

1 tsp Chopped thyme

1 Bay leaf

½ tsp Black peppercorns

½ tsp Juniper berries

Dry Cure, see ***curing***

STAGE 1

1. To prepare the wings, chop off the tip and bottom of the wing leaving the centre part with 2 bones inside it.

2. Sprinkle the ***dry cure*** over the wings and leave in the fridge for 12 hours.

STAGE 2

3. Pre-heat your water bath to 75°C.

4. Take the chicken out of the fridge and rinse under cold running water for 10 minutes. Then pat dry with kitchen towel.

5. Place the chicken and all other ingredients into a pouch and vac-seal.

Depending on the size of your pouches, you might want to seal the wings individually.

6. Now, put the pouches into your water bath for 4 hours.

7. Keep checking the water bath to make sure the water is covering the pouches.

8. When the time is up place the chicken into ice water for 2 minutes.

9. Remove the chicken wings from the pouches and whilst still warm, gently remove the bones from the meat by pushing them up and out.

10. Now, put the chicken into the fridge until cold.

11. Finish the wings in a hot pan and serve immediately.

To regenerate from cold pan fry the chicken wings to give a crispy outside and beautiful flavoursome inside.

Chef's Tip —
Leave the wings whole and marinade in masala butter, then sous vide as above and roast off.

4 hrs
75°C
Four
3
Med
— Dish Suggestion —
Slow Cooked Crispy Chicken Wings.

Turkey Breast

26

Injecting the turkey breast with butter is so simple, yet so effective. Making the meat tender, moist and succulent — you'll be doing this every time you cook turkey.

INGREDIENTS

1 Turkey breast, 1½kg

6 Smoked bacon rashers

1 Chicken stock cube

Salt

Pepper

Orange and Chestnut Butter, see ***butters***

For this recipe you will need a large syringe/basting needle.

METHOD

1. Pre-heat your water bath to 65°C.

2. Melt down the ***orange and chestnut butter*** and with the syringe, inject it deep into the flesh of the turkey breast – keep some of the butter back to cover the outside of the breast later.

3. Season the breast with the stock cube, salt and pepper.

4. Now, put the turkey in a pouch, along with the rest of the butter and smoked bacon, and vac-seal.

5. Place the pouch into your water bath for 7 hours.

6. Keep checking the water bath to make sure the water is covering the pouch.

7. Remove the turkey from the pouch and pat dry with kitchen towel.

8. Roast the skin on both sides until golden and crisp, serve immediately.

You can place the pouch in ice water and then leave in the fridge for up to three days.

To regenerate from cold place the pouch in your water bath for 1 hour 30 minutes at 60°C and finish by roasting the skin on both sides.

Chef's Tip —
The turkey can be done in advance, 'regenerated' and re-heated at 60° C for 1 hour 30 minutes.

7 hrs
65°C
Four
3
Med
– Dish Suggestion –
Christmas Turkey with Traditional Trimmings.

27

Pheasant

Sous vide cooking pheasant produces something so tender and moist that you'll be tempted to sneak a bit while it's resting.

INGREDIENTS

2 Pheasant breasts

50g Pancetta or bacon fat

1 Thyme sprig

100g Girolles mushrooms — or any wild variety

50g Butter

METHOD

1. Pre-heat your water bath to 62°C.

2. Place the pheasant breasts and pancetta/bacon fat into a pouch, along with the thyme, and vac-seal.

3. Put the pouch into your water bath for 35 minutes.

4. Keep checking the water bath to make sure the water is covering the pouch.

5. Remove the pheasant from the pouch and pat dry with kitchen towel.

6. Colour the pheasant in a pan, skin side down only, until crispy.

7. Now, add the girolles to the pan, along with a tablespoon of butter, and allow to foam — glazing the pheasant and mushrooms with the butter.

8. Remove the pheasant from pan and let it rest for 4 minutes.

9. Carve and serve.

Chef's Tip —
Use chestnuts for a sauce, quince can be used as a purée or butternut squash is great as well.

35 mins
62°C
Two
2
Easy
— Dish Suggestion —
Roasted Pheasant, Winter Cabbage and Apple.

28

Pigeon

Pigeon is often overcooked, resulting in dry meat, but we're going to change that here. The resulting flavour and tenderness is enhanced with the sweet blackberries and salty pancetta.

INGREDIENTS

4 Pigeon breasts – fillet removed

Salt to taste

4 Pancetta rashers

1 Thyme sprig

1 Punnet blackberries

250ml Sloe gin

250ml Red wine

10g Sugar

METHOD

1. Pre-heat your water bath to 55°C.

2. Ask your butcher to remove the pigeon breasts from the carcass, or if you are confident then do this yourself.

3. Place the pigeon breasts and one pancetta rasher into a pouch and vac-seal.

4. In a hot pan add the sloe gin, red wine and sugar. When it reaches a boil burn the alcohol off with a naked flame.

5. Reduce the liquid to a syrup and allow to cool to room temperature.

6. Place the blackberries in a pouch, along with the thyme, add the syrup and vac-seal. If you have an external vacuum sealer either vacuum seal using a zip lock bag instead or freeze the syrup in an ice cube tray and add to the bag before vacuum sealing with your external sealer.

7. Put both pouches into your water bath for 15 minutes.

8. Keep checking the water bath to make sure the water is covering the pouches.

9. Remove the pigeon from the pouch and pat dry with kitchen towel.

10. Colour the pigeon, skin side down in a hot pan until crispy, season and remove from the pan allowing it to rest.

11. Grill the remaining pancetta until nice and crispy.

12. Drain off blackberries and plate up.

Chef's Tip –
Try pheasant instead of pigeon, set the sloe gin liquid with gelatine at a ratio of 100ml liquid to 1 leaf to make a jelly.

15 mins
55°C
Two
5
Hard
— Dish Suggestion —
Wood Pigeon, Sloe Gin Poached Blackberries and Pancetta.

29

Duck Supreme

Duck and orange is a classic combination, bringing a faint zing that works really well with the honey and marmalade. Crispy skin and juicy flesh never tasted so good.

INGREDIENTS

4 Duck supremes, each 200g

50g Marmalade – good quality

Zest of ½ orange

1 tbsp Honey

1 tsp Thyme leaves

½ tsp Sea salt

METHOD

1. Pre-heat your water bath to 54°C for rare, or 57°C for medium.

2. In a bowl, mix the orange zest, thyme, sea salt, honey and marmalade.

3. Trim the duck supremes of all their sinew and excess skin, then score the skin with a sharp knife.

4. On the flesh side only, brush on the just mixed zesty marinade.

5. Now, put the duck supremes in a pouch and vac-seal.

Depending on the size of your pouches, you might want to seal the supremes individually.

6. Place the pouches into your water bath for 1 hour 30 minutes.

7. Keep checking the water bath to make sure the water is covering the pouches.

8. Remove the duck from the pouches and pat dry with kitchen towel.

9. Cook the breast off in a dry pan, skin side down to give a crispy finish.

Or you can place the pouches in ice water until cold and keep in the fridge for up to three days.

To regenerate from cold place the pouches in your water bath for 20 minutes at 57°C and seal in a pan, skin side down.

Chef's Tip –
Any other flavour can be added to the bag – try maple syrup.

1½ hrs
54°C
Four
5
Hard
— Dish Suggestion —
Roast Duck Supreme with Beetroot and Pomegranate.

30

Confit Leg of Duck

A world away from crispy duck and pancakes, the legs take on the herb and orange flavours wonderfully.

INGREDIENTS

4 Duck legs

1 tsp Chopped thyme leaves

1 Bay leaf

Zest of 1 orange

Dry Cure, see ***curing***

STAGE 1

1. Remove any excess fat from the duck legs and chop off the knuckle of the leg bone with a sharp knife.

2. Cover both sides of the leg with the ***dry cure*** and store in the fridge for 12 hours.

STAGE 2

3. Pre-heat your water bath to 82°C.

4. Remove the duck legs from the cure and rinse under cold running water for 10 minutes, pat dry with kitchen towel.

5. Now, put the duck legs in a pouch along with the thyme leaves, bay leaf and orange zest and vac-seal.

Depending on the size of your pouches, you might want to seal the legs individually, if this is the case distribute the dry ingredients evenly between the bags.

6. Place the pouches into your water bath for 8 hours.

7. Keep checking the water bath to make sure the water is covering the pouches.

8. Remove the duck from the pouches and pop in a hot pan to crisp the skin. The duck legs are now ready to serve.

9. You can place the pouches in ice water until cold and keep in the fridge for up to three days.

To regenerate from cold pan roast the duck legs for crispy skin and place in hot oven for 10 minutes.

Chef's Tip —
Brush the duck legs with honey or the preserved orange cure recipe instead of the dry cure.

8 hrs
82°C
Four
4
Med
— Dish Suggestion —
Confit Duck, Charred Cabbage and Braised Hibiscus Beetroot.

31

Ox Cheek

Becoming more and more fashionable, ox cheek lends itself perfectly to sous vide cooking. The resulting flesh is soft, tender and so full of flavour it's a thing of majesty.

INGREDIENTS

4 Ox cheeks, each 200g

1 Bottle of red wine

3 Sprigs of thyme

2 tbsp Brown sugar

1 tsp salt

10 Peppercorns

2 Shallots – sliced thinly

6 Garlic cloves – crushed

1 Bay leaf

2 tbsp Bovril or beef extract

1 Pint beef stock

Dry Cure, see ***curing***

STAGE 1

1. Cover your ox cheeks with the ***dry cure*** and store in the fridge for 12 hours.

STAGE 2

2. Pre-heat your water bath to 80°C.

3. Seal the ox cheeks in a thick bottomed pan to get some lovely carmelisation.

4. Sauté the shallots, garlic, bay leaf, peppercorns and thyme until the shallots turn translucent.

5. Add the wine, sugar, salt, bovril and reduce by half.

6. Then add the pint of stock, and again reduce by half for intense flavour.

7. Allow the sauce to cool.

STAGE 3

8. Place the ox cheeks and sauce in a pouch and vac-seal. If using an external vacuum sealer create a vacuum using a zip lock bag instead.

Depending on the size of your pouches, you might want to seal the cheeks individually or in pairs.

9. Place the pouches into your water bath for 15 hours.

10. Keep checking the water bath to make sure the water is covering the pouches.

11. Remove the ox cheeks from the pouches and serve.

12. You can place the pouches in ice water until cold and keep in the fridge for up to three days.

To regenerate from cold place the pouches in your water bath at 75°C for 50 minutes.

Chef's Tip —
Smoke the ox cheeks and cook without the stock.

4
15 hrs
80°C
Two
Med
— Dish Suggestion —
Cider Braised Pork Cheeks, Parsnip Purée and Honey Glazed Baby Parsnips.

32

Fillet of Beef

Beef fillet only needs to be cooked simply, the tenderness achieved through sous vide cooking creates a melt-in-the-mouth experience you won't forget.

INGREDIENTS

4 Beef fillet portions, each 180g — trimmed fully

½ tsp Sea salt

1 tsp Chopped thyme leaves

2 tbsp Truffle butter — see ***butters***

METHOD

1. Pre-heat your water bath to 56°C.

2. Trim all the sinew off the beef fillet then season with salt and chopped thyme.

If the fillet portions are from the tail end you can wrap them tightly in cling film to keep the cylindrical shape.

3. Place each fillet in a pouch, along with equal amounts of truffle butter, and vac-seal.

4. Now, put the pouches into your water bath for 25 minutes.

5. Keep checking the water bath to make sure the water is covering the pouches.

6. Remove the beef fillets from the pouches and pat dry with kitchen towel.

7. Finish the fillets off in a hot pan to give some extra colour and flavour.

8. You can place the pouches in ice water until cold and keep in the fridge for up to three days.

To regenerate from cold place the pouches in your water bath at 55°C for 12 minutes, then finish in a hot pan.

Chef's Tip —
Why not brush the fillet with treacle and thyme to add depth of flavour.

25 mins
56°C
Four
4
Med
— Dish Suggestion —
Truffled Fillet of Beef, Roasted Onion and Wild Mushrooms.

33

Rib Eye Steak

Simple, quick and perfect every time the cooked rib eye is absolutely bursting with fresh herb flavour.

INGREDIENTS

2 Rib eye steaks, each 220g

½ tsp Sea salt

20ml Olive oil

½ tsp Thyme or tarragon
– chopped

METHOD

When purchasing your steak, make sure it has good marbling throughout. This will ensure your have lots of flavour.

1. Pre-heat your water bath to 55°C for rare, or 58°C for medium rare.

2. Season the steaks on both sides and sprinkle with your chosen herbs.

3. Place the steaks in a pouch and vac-seal.

Depending on the size of your pouches, you might want to seal them individually.

6. Now, put the pouches into your water bath for 45 minutes at your desired temperature.

7. Keep checking the water bath to make sure the water is covering the pouches.

8. Remove the steaks from the pouches and pat dry with kitchen towel.

9. Brush the steaks with oil, season again and char-grill before serving.

Or you can place the pouches in ice water until cold and keep in the fridge for up to three days.

To regenerate from cold place the pouches in the water bath for 12 minutes at 55°C, finishing in a hot pan before serving.

Chef's Tip —
Add bone marrow to the bag to intensify the beef flavour.

45 mins
55°C
Two
1
Easy
— Dish Suggestion —
Char-grilled Rib Eye and
Triple Cooked Chips.

34

Sirloin of Beef

Sunday lunch won't be the same again once you've tried this sirloin of beef. The meat is so tender it's effortless to carve leaving you to worry if you have space around the table.

INGREDIENTS

1½kg Piece of sirloin – trimmed

2 tbsp Thyme leaves – chopped

2 tbsp Sea salt

½ tsp Ground black pepper

3 tsp Olive oil

METHOD

1. Pre-heat your water bath to 55°C.

2. Trim off any sinew and excess fat or ask your butcher to prepare it for you.

3. Gently score the top of the fat on the sirloin, this will release some fat and help render it down ready for later.

4. Season the sirloin all over and sprinkle the thyme over the fat.

5. Place the sirloin in a large pouch and vac-seal.

6. Now, put the pouch into your water bath for 6 hours for medium rare.

7. Keep checking the water bath to make sure the water is covering the pouches.

8. Remove the sirloin from the pouch, pat dry with kitchen towel and allow to rest for 5 minutes.

9. Finish the sirloin in a hot pan on all sides until brown all over. Rest for a further 5 minutes to allow the meat to relax and become tender.

Slice and serve immediately.

10. You can place the pouch in ice water until cold and keep in the fridge for up to three days.

To regenerate from cold place the pouch in your water bath at 55°C for 2 hours, then finish in a hot pan.

Chef's Tip –
Try adding pancetta, flavoured butters or charred onions to the bag.

6 hrs
55°C
Four
2
Easy
— Dish Suggestion —
Sunday Roast Beef
with all the Trimmings.

35

Rump Cap of Beef

Also known as 'picanha' this cut of beef is popular in Brazil as it's very tasty and tender.

INGREDIENTS

4 Rump caps, each 180g – thick square cut

1 Beef stock cube

100g Dried mushrooms – ground to a powder

½ tsp Salt

1 tsp Olive oil

METHOD

1. Pre-heat your water bath to 55°C.

2. Gently score the fat on top of the rump cap portions.

3. Crumble the stock cube up and mix with the salt, dried ground mushrooms and olive oil to form a paste.

4. Rub the paste all over the rump cap – over the fat as well as the meat.

5. Place the rump caps in a pouch and vac-seal.

Depending on the size of your pouches, you might want to seal them individually.

6. Now, pop the pouches into your water bath for 2 hours for medium rare or 1 hour 45 minutes for rare.

7. Keep checking the water bath to make sure the water is covering the pouches.

8. Remove the rump caps from the pouches and pat dry with kitchen towel.

9. Brown the fat side in a medium heated pan and then colour the other sides. Allow to rest for 5 minutes.

Slice and serve immediately.

10. You can place the pouch in ice water until cold and keep in the fridge for up to three days.

To regenerate from cold place the pouches in your water bath at 55°C for 45 minutes, then finish in a medium heated pan.

Chef's Tip – Try smoking the rump before Sous Vide.

2 hrs
55°C
Four
3
Med
— Dish Suggestion —
Mushroom Scented Rump of Beef, Mash and Burgundy Jus.

36

Beef Onglet

Onglet, or hanger steak, is a little known cut of beef, that has been savoured in France for years. It's more economical and flavoursome than fillet.

INGREDIENTS

1kg Beef onglet

1 Beef stock cube

¼ tsp Black pepper

½ tsp Sea salt

½ tsp Marjoram — chopped

METHOD

1. Pre-heat your water bath to 57°C.

2. Trim any excess sinew from the outside of the beef and cut into 200g portions.

3. In a bowl mix the powdered stock cube, pepper, salt and chopped marjoram.

4. Roll the beef portions in the aromatic powdered crust.

5. Place the beef in a pouch and vac-seal.

Depending on the size of your pouches, you might want to seal the beef individually or in pairs.

6. Now, put the pouches into your water bath for 26 hours.

7. Keep checking the water bath to make sure the water is covering the pouches.

8. Remove the beef from the pouches and finish in a hot pan for a lovely crust on the outside.

9. You can place the pouches in ice water until cold and keep in the fridge for up to three days.

To regenerate from cold place the pouches in your water bath at 57°C for 1 hour, then finish in a hot pan.

Chef's Tip —
Why not smoke the onglet portions to give an authentic BBQ flavour.

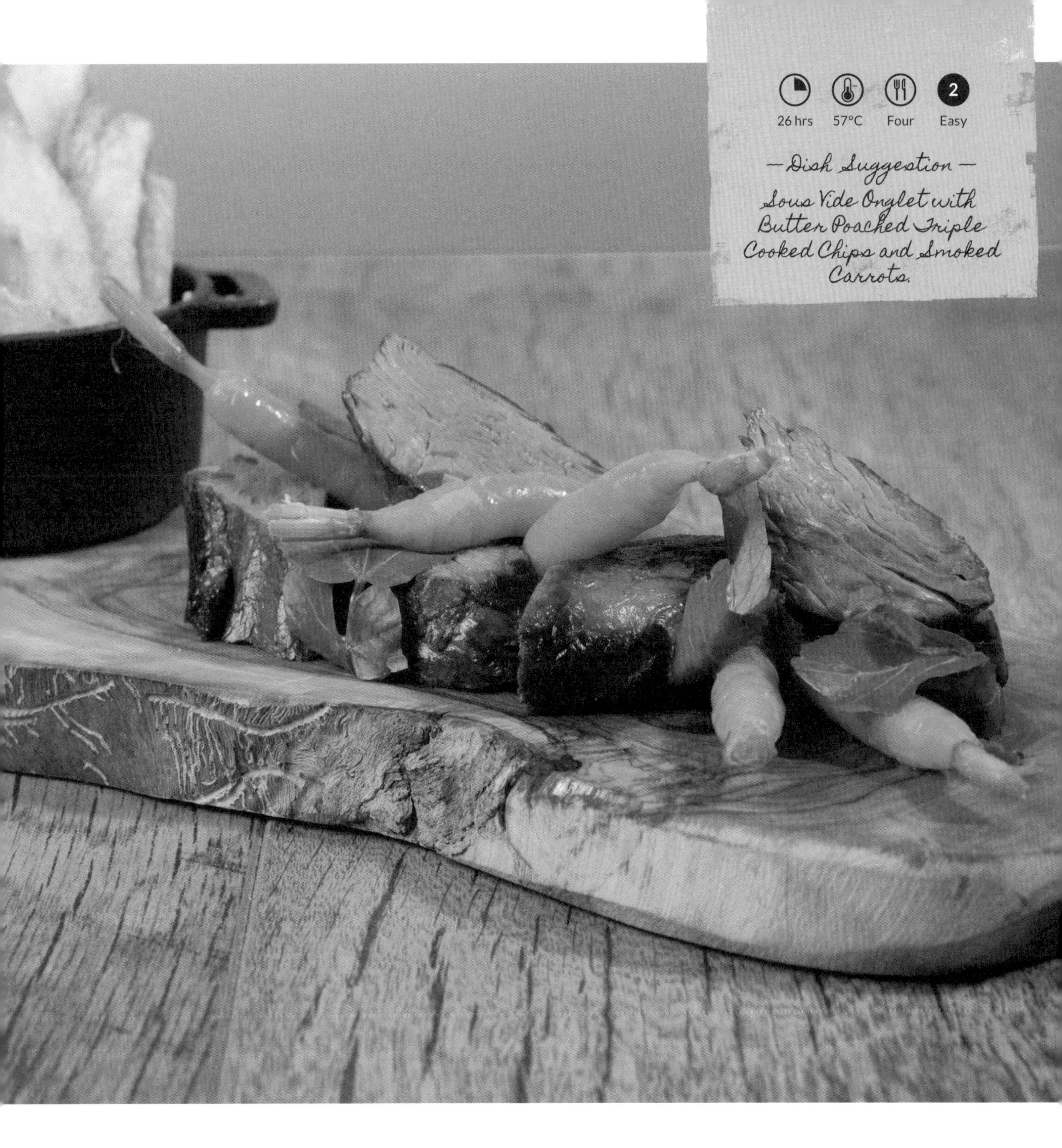
26 hrs
57°C
Four
2
Easy
– Dish Suggestion –
Sous Vide Onglet with Butter Poached Triple Cooked Chips and Smoked Carrots.

37

Beef Burger

The chuck and brisket combine perfectly to make the most awesome burger you'll ever have. The flavours speak for themselves with these homemade beauties.

INGREDIENTS

1kg Chuck beef — diced/minced

250g Brisket — diced/minced

250g Marrowbone fat — minced

Salt

Pepper

METHOD

1. Pre-heat your water bath to 60°C.

2. Ask your butcher to mince 1kg chuck beef with the marrowbone fat and beef brisket — or you can do it yourself.

3. Mix all the ingredients and season with the salt and pepper.

4. Form the mixture into burger portions using a ring mould for consistency.

5. Store your fledgling burgers in the fridge until firm.

6. Place each burger in a pouch and vac-seal.

7. Put all the pouches into your water bath for 1 hour until medium rare.

8. Keep checking the water bath to make sure the water is covering the pouches.

9. Remove the pouches from the water bath and place in ice water until cold.

10. Then, remove the burgers from the pouches and finish in a hot pan on both sides until lovely and brown.

11. You can keep the pouches in the fridge for up to three days and finish later if needed — perfect for parties.

To regenerate from cold place the pouches in your water bath at 60°C for 20 minutes, then finish in a pan or BBQ.

Chef's Tip —
Cold smoke the burger after it has set in the fridge, then cook or BBQ.

3
1 hr
60°C
Four
Med
– Dish Suggestion –
Classic Beef Burger, Relish and Triple Cooked Chips.

38

Spiced Lamb Meatballs

This dish is great for people who want a finished dish at the end of the sous vide process. All the ingredients go into the pouch together making all the preparation worth the wait.

INGREDIENTS

1kg Lamb — minced

1½ Red onions — finely chopped

1½ Cloves garlic — crushed

1 Red chilli — seeded and finely chopped

1 Egg

1½ tsp Mild curry powder

1 tsp Chilli flakes

25g Coriander — chopped

1½ tsp Toasted cumin seeds — crushed

Zest of ½ orange

1 tsp Smoked paprika

50g Dried apricots — finely chopped

25g Toasted pinenuts

½ tsp Salt

¼ tsp White ground pepper

200ml Tomato passata

75g Red lentils

100ml Olive oil

STAGE 1

1. Pre-heat your water bath to 55°C.

2. Put a pan of oil onto heat and soften the onions, garlic and chilli until the onion is translucent.

3. Next, add all the spices, apricots, nuts and orange zest to the pan. You'll need to sauté this for a further 10 minutes.

4. Once done, leave to cool on the side.

5. When your mixture is cool, add your minced lamb, salt and pepper and bind with 1 egg. You're now ready to shape your meatballs, aim for around 50g each if you can.

6. Place the finished meatballs on a plate and leave to set in the fridge.

STAGE 2

7. Place your lentils, tomato passata and salt into a pouch, then get your meatballs from the fridge and carefully add those.

8. Vac-seal the pouch and place in your water bath for 24 hours. If you have an external vacuum sealer use a zip lock bag to create a vacuum instead.

9. Keep checking the water bath to make sure the water is covering the pouch.

10. Remove the pouch from the water bath and serve.

11. You can keep the pouch in the fridge for up to three days and finish later if needed — perfect for parties.

To regenerate from cold heat the meatballs in a pan with the sauce.

Chef's Tip —
Try the same method using pork mince, veal mince, or beef mince.

24 hrs
55°C
Four
4
Med
— Dish Suggestion —
Spiced Lamb Meatballs
with Cous Cous and
Cucumber Raita

39

Butterflied Leg of Lamb

The delicious dry spiced mix turns the leg of lamb into a gorgeous, aromatic experience you'll want to try again and again.

INGREDIENTS

2kg Leg Lamb – boned

DRY SPICE MIX INGREDIENTS

Dry roast and grind to a powder.

1 tsp Cumin

2 Cardamom pods

1 tsp Coriander

1 tsp Cinnamon

1 tsp Dried chilli flakes

½ tsp Pepper corns

1 tsp Salt

1 tsp Garlic powder

1 tsp Onion powder

METHOD

1. Pre-heat your water bath to 65°C.

2. Open the leg of lamb and score the inside with a knife.

3. Dust heavily with the dry spiced mix.

4. Place your lamb into a pouch and vac-seal.

5. Put the pouch into your water bath for 4 hours.

6. Keep checking the water bath to make sure the water is covering the pouch.

7. Remove the pouch from the water bath and finish the lamb on a BBQ or in a griddle pan.

8. Rest the lamb for 5 minutes before carving and serving.

9. You can place the pouch in ice water until cold and keep in the fridge for up to three days.

To regenerate from cold place the pouch in your water bath at 65°C for 1 hour and finish on a BBQ or in a griddle pan.

Chef's Tip —
Any form of marinade can be used: masala, mint and basil, tomato.

4 hrs
65°C
Six
4
Med
— Dish Suggestion —
BBQ Sous Vide Leg of Lamb,
Mint and Basil Purée
and Tomato Tabouleu.

Lamb Sweetbreads

40

The delicacy in flavour and smooth, soft texture of lamb sweetbreads is the perfect partner to the herb scented rosemary flour that creates a crisp finish.

INGREDIENTS

300g Fresh lamb sweetbreads

1 litre Milk

FLOUR INGREDIENTS

Blend together to create Rosemary Flour.

100g Soft flour

25g Rosemary

Salt

Pepper

METHOD

1. Pre-heat your water bath to 62°C.

2. First soak the sweetbreads in half of the milk for 8 hours.

3. Bring 2 pints of water to boil – quickly blanch the sweetbreads for 10 seconds – then chill immediately on ice.

4. Peel off any excess sinew.

5. Place the cleaned sweetbreads, and the remaining milk in a pouch and vac-seal. If you have an external vacuum sealer use a zip lock bag to create a vacuum instead.

6. Put the pouch into your water bath for 40 minutes.

7. Keep checking the water bath to make sure the water is covering the pouch.

8. Remove the sweetbreads from the pouch and pat dry with kitchen towel.

9. Now, roll in the rosemary flour and pan fry until crisp – serve immediately.

10. You can place the pouch in ice water until cold and keep in the fridge for up to three days.

To regenerate from cold place the pouch in your water bath at 62°C for 30 minutes.

Chef's Tip –
Try adding spice instead of rosemary to the flour or spice to the pouch instead of milk before cooking.

40 mins
62°C
Two
3
Med
— Dish Suggestion —
Roasted Lambs Sweetbreads with Charred Leeks and Dried Tomato.

41

Lamb Neck Fillets

We all know that mint goes well with lamb, and pairing that with basil really makes for a taste sensation when utilising this delicious and inexpensive cut.

INGREDIENTS

4 Lamb neck fillets, each 220g

5 Mint leaves

5 Basil leaves

Salt

Pepper

METHOD

1. Pre-heat your water bath to 55°C.

2. Trim any excess sinew from the neck fillets then season with salt and pepper.

3. Wrap each neck in 5 mint and 5 basil leaves.

4. Place each neck fillet into individual pouches and vac-seal.

5. Put the pouches into your water bath for 24 hours – this recipe keeps the neck nice and pink unlike traditional braising.

6. Keep checking the water bath to make sure the water is covering the pouches.

7. Remove the neck fillets from the pouches and finish in a hot pan to create a rich roasted flavour.

8. You can place the pouches in ice water until cold and keep in the fridge for up to three days.

To regenerate from cold place the pouch in your water bath at 55°C for 30 minutes.

*Chef's Tip —
Roll the necks in tomato powder or sundried tomatoes.*

24 hrs
55°C
Four
4
Med
— Dish Suggestion —
Slow Cooked Lamb Neck Fillet, Peas, Goats Cheese and Cumin Yoghurt.

Lamb Breast

42

Another one of the least expensive cuts of lamb, breast is full of delicious flavour but needs cooking long and slow — perfect for sous vide cooking. You'll love the finished texture of the meat.

INGREDIENTS

1 Whole breast of lamb — boned and rolled

50g Chopped mint

30g Chopped rosemary

75g Castor sugar

75g Salt

STAGE 1

1. Lay your lamb breast in a tray.

2. In a blender combine the mint, rosemary, sugar and salt to make a dry rub.

3. Cover the lamb breast with the rub and refrigerate for 12 hours.

STAGE 2

4. Pre-heat your water bath to 82°C.

5. Rinse the lamb under cold running water to remove all the rub.

6. Then, place into a pouch and vac-seal.

7. Put the pouch into your water bath for 16 hours.

8. Keep checking the water bath to make sure the water is covering the pouch.

9. After 16 hours, remove the lamb breast from its pouch and roll in cling film to give a uniformed shape. Place in the fridge overnight.

10. Cut the lamb into around 200g portions and pan fry both sides until delicious and crisp.

Chef's Tip —
You can smoke the breast after the curing process.

3
16 hrs
82°C
Four
Med
– Dish Suggestion –
Crispy Lamb Breast with Smoked Tomatoes and Broad Bean Vinaigrette.

43

Rump of Lamb

The flavour contained in the rump is amazing, and sous vide cooking helps to push that flavour through all the meat. The olive purée adds a subtle saltiness for extra depth.

INGREDIENTS

4 Lamb rumps, each 200g

40g Tomato purée

50g Olive purée, or tapenade

1 Sprig rosemary

Salt

Pepper

METHOD

1. Pre-heat your water bath to 62°C.

2. Cross hatch the fat side of the lamb rumps.

3. On the flesh side only — season the lamb with salt and pepper, and rub on the tomato and olive purée.

4. Place each rump into an individual pouch, add equal amounts of rosemary, and vac-seal.

5. Put the pouches into your water bath for 45 minutes.

6. Keep checking the water bath to make sure the water is covering the pouches.

7. Remove the lamb rumps from the pouches and pat dry with kitchen towel.

8. You can place the pouches in ice water until cold and keep in the fridge for up to three days if required.

9. In a hot pan seal the fat side until nice and crispy, seasoning with salt and pepper.

10. Seal the other side of the lamb for colour and you're ready to serve.

To regenerate from cold place the pouches in your water bath at 62°C for 25 minutes.

Chef's Tip —
Rub the flesh side with garlic powder and lemon zest.

45 mins
62°C
Four
3
Med
— Dish Suggestion —
Rump of Lamb, Charred Pimento, Grilled Courgette and Smoked Pinenuts.

44

Loin of Lamb

Wrapping the loin of lamb in hay adds a wonderful grassy flavour to the meat that has to be experienced.

INGREDIENTS

4 Loin of lamb portions, each 200g – fully trimmed

100g Edible hay

¼ tsp Onion granules

¼ tsp Garlic powder

Zest of ½ lemon

METHOD

1. Pre-heat your water bath to 55°C.

2. Mix the onion granules, garlic powder and lemon zest together, rub into all sides of the lamb loins.

3. Wet the hay and wrap it around the lamb loin portions.

4. Place the hay-wrapped lamb loins into a pouch and vac-seal.

Depending on the size of your pouches, you might want to seal the lamb individually or in pairs.

5. Put the pouches into your water bath for 25 minutes.

6. Keep checking the water bath to make sure the water is covering the pouches.

7. Remove the lamb from the pouches and discard the hay.

8. You can place the pouches in ice water until cold and keep in the fridge for up to three days.

9. Seal the lamb pieces on all sides in a hot pan with a little oil and season to taste with salt and pepper.

To regenerate from cold place the pouches in your water bath at 55°C for 15 minutes.

Chef's Tip –
Try cooking the loins in natural yoghurt and lemon zest to add a fresh taste to the lamb.

25 mins
55°C
Four
4
Med
— Dish Suggestion —
Hay Roasted Lamb Loin,
Smoked Onions and Butter
Poached Carrots.

Smoked Best End of Lamb

45

A simple presentation of best end of lamb. A delicate smoked flavour, with not too many ingredients, helps to create something quite amazing.

INGREDIENTS

8 Bone best end of lamb
— French trimmed and smoked

6 Basil leaves

Salt

Pepper

PolyScience smoking gun

Smoking chips

METHOD

1. Pre-heat your water bath to 65°C.

2. Place the rack of lamb in an air tight container and season with salt and pepper.

3. Using the PolyScience smoking gun fill the container with smoke, replace the lid and put in the fridge for 30 minutes — repeat this process six times.

4. After the sixth time, season the lamb, place into a pouch and vac-seal.

5. Put the pouch into your water bath for 1 hour 30 minutes.

6. Keep checking the water bath to make sure the water is covering the pouches.

7. Remove the lamb from the pouch and pat dry with kitchen towel.

8. You can place the pouches in ice water until cold and keep in the fridge for up to three days.

9. Roast the lamb in a pan on all sides, allow to rest for 5 minutes and carve to serve.

To regenerate from cold place the pouches in your water bath at 65°C for 30 minutes.

Chef's Tip —
Rub the lamb with garlic powder and the addition of mint instead of smoking.

1½ hrs
65°C
Four
4
Med
— Dish Suggestion —
Smoked Best End of Lamb with Roasted Vegetables.

46

Shoulder of Lamb

A decent shoulder of lamb is always impressive however you cook it — this way is simple, tasty and really shows off the meat.

INGREDIENTS

2kg Shoulder of lamb — boned

150g Masala Butter, see ***butters***

Dry Cure, see ***curing***

METHOD

1. Pre-heat your water bath to 56°C.

2. Open up the shoulder of lamb — 'butterfly' — and make small ½cm cuts on the flesh side.

3. Heavily season the shoulder with the ***dry cure*** and refrigerate for 12 hours.

4. After 12 hours, rinse the lamb under cold running water to remove all of the dry cure, pat dry with kitchen towel.

At this point re-tie the shoulder to its original shape.

5. Cover the lamb in the ***masala butter,*** put in a pouch and vac-seal.

6. Place the pouch into your water bath for 72 hours.

7. Keep checking the water bath to make sure the water is covering the pouch.

8. Remove the shoulder of lamb from the pouch and finish off on a BBQ or in a griddle pan.

9. You can place the pouch in ice water until cold and keep in the fridge for up to three days.

To regenerate from cold place the pouch in your water bath at 56°C for 1 hour 30 minutes and finish on a BBQ or griddle pan.

Chef's Tip —
Use sun-dried tomatoes and basil, blended to a paste instead of the masala butter.

72 hrs
56°C
Six
5
Hard
— Dish Suggestion —
BBQ Spiced Lamb with Garden Herb Salad.

Venison Loin

47

Venison is a fantastic lean dark meat — it can be just as succulent and juicy as any cut of beef — and lends itself perfectly to sweet berry flavours.

INGREDIENTS

4 Venison loin portions, each 200g

50g Hibiscus dried flower

25g Pink peppercorns

2 tsp Chopped thyme

Pinch of sea salt

4 tbsp Wild honey

METHOD

1. Pre-heat your water bath to 55°C.

2. Trim off any sinew from the venison loin so it is just lean meat.

3. Gently warm the honey and brush all over the loin.

4. Place the venison in a pouch and vac-seal.

6. Now, put the pouch into your water bath for 1 hour.

7. Keep checking the water bath to make sure the water is covering the pouch.

8. In a small hand blender or pestle and mortar, grind the pink peppercorns and dried hibiscus flowers with the thyme to a powder – then add the sea salt.

9. Remove the venison from the pouch and roll in the hibiscus peppercorn powder.

10. Then, colour in a medium heated pan – because the venison has been cooked in honey – and allow to rest for 5 minutes.

11. Carve and serve immediately. A blackberry sauce will work really well with the venison.

Chef's Tip —
Cook with marmalade, orange zest and sage.

4
1 hr
55°C
Four
Med
—Dish Suggestion—
Roasted Venison with
Hibiscus and Peppercorn,
Blackberry Jus.

Onions, Leeks, Carrots,
Parsnips, Corn, Fennel,
Asparagus, Cauliflower,
Mushrooms, Pumpkin,
Beetroot and Eggs.

Accompaniments

Boiling vegetables in salted water has been the tradition for hundreds of years, but this has a massive disadvantage as flavour is lost from the cells of the vegetable and are replaced with flavourless water.

In this section we look at new and slower ways of approaching this subject. For example a carrot cooked in its own carrot juice has to taste of carrot, and at low temperature the vegetables cannot be overcooked. The flavour transfer between just a few ingredients really makes for some amazing flavours — what's in the bag, stays in the bag.

2½ hrs

86°C

Four

Easy

Roasted Onions

INGREDIENTS

3 Small white onions

2 Bay leaves

Pinch star anise powder

1 tbsp Caster sugar

½ tsp Sea salt

200 ml Chicken stock, optional

20ml Wine vinegar

Olive oil

METHOD

1. Pre-heat your water bath to 86°C.

2. Peel the onions and slice 1cm thick.

3. Caramelise one side of the onion until golden brown in a little olive oil.

4. Mix all the other ingredients in a bowl and place in the pouch, along with the onion slices, and vac-seal. If using an external vacuum sealer do not include the optional chicken stock.

5. Now, put the pouch into your water bath for 2 hours 30 minutes.

6. Keep checking the water bath to make sure the water is covering the pouches.

7. When finished, place the pouch in ice water until cold and keep in the fridge for up to three days.

To regenerate from cold heat the onions in an oven at 160°C for 10 minutes.

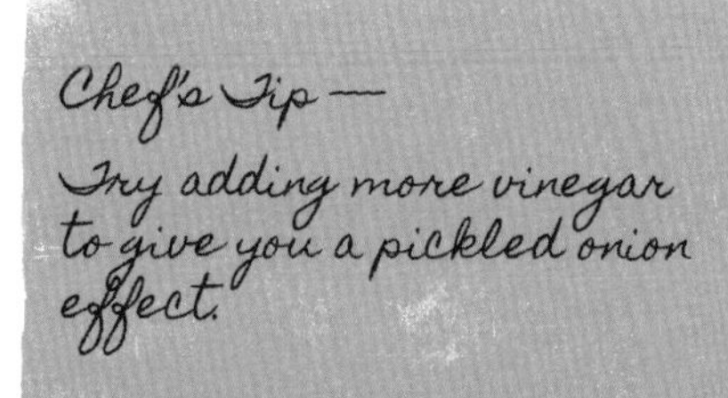

1½ hrs

75°C

Four

Med

49 Smoked Onions

INGREDIENTS

200g Silverskin onions

4 Rashers pancetta

½ tsp Thyme

Salt

Pepper

PolyScience smoking gun

Smoking chips

METHOD

1. Pre-heat your water bath to 75°C.

2. Place a pan of salted water on to boil. Once you have a rapid boil, add the silverskin onions and cook until just going tender.

3. Carefully put the onions in ice water for 10 seconds so still warm but cold enough to handle.

4. Peel the skin off with a small knife.

5. When the onions are peeled, add all the onions to an airtight container or under a glass cloche.

6. Smoke and leave for 10 minutes, repeating the process 7 or 8 times.

7. When smoked, place the onions, pancetta and thyme in a large pouch and vac-seal.

8. Put the pouch into your water bath for 1 hour 30 minutes.

9. Keep checking the water bath to make sure the water is covering the pouches.

10. When finished, place the pouch in ice water until cold and keep in the fridge for up to three days.

Chef's Tip —
Add 45 ml of the pickling liquor to onions when placing in the poach to give a pickled/ smoked flavour.

1½ hrs

88°C

Two

Easy

50

Truffle Leeks

INGREDIENTS

6 Medium sized leeks

1 tbsp Sugar

1 tsp Salt

2 tbsp White truffle cream

50ml Duck fat

50ml White wine

10ml Cider vinegar

1 tsp Chopped thyme

METHOD

1. Pre-heat your water bath to 88°C.

2. Trim your leeks of the top green leaves and wash in iced water.

3. Place in a 300cm pouch along with the other ingredients and vac-seal.

4. Put the pouch into your water bath for 1 hour 30 minutes, or 2 hours depending on the size of your leeks.

5. Keep checking the water bath to make sure the water is covering the pouch.

6. Once the time is up, finish the leeks off in a hot pan.

7. You can place the pouch in ice water until cold and keep in the fridge for up to three days.

Pan roast the cold leeks and reheat in the oven at 180°C for 10 minutes.

Chef's Tip —
Try adding 100g of smoked pancetta to give a smoked bacon flavour to the leeks.

1 hr 45

88°C

Two

Easy

Baby Carrots

INGREDIENTS

2 Baby carrots bunches

1 tbsp Sugar

150ml Carrot juice

½ tsp Sea salt

Pinch of thyme

METHOD

1. Pre-heat your water bath to 88°C.

2. Prepare the carrots by snipping off the tops and washing thoroughly.

3. Whisk the other ingredients in a bowl, place in a 300cm pouch along with the carrots and vac-seal. If you have an external vacuum sealer either vacuum seal using a zip lock bag instead or freeze the juice in an ice cube tray and add to the bag before vacuum sealing with your external vacuum sealer.

4. Put the pouch into your water bath for 50 minutes, or 1 hour 45 minutes depending on the size of your carrots.

5. Keep checking the water bath to make sure the water is covering the pouch.

6. Remove the carrots from the pouch and serve.

7. You can place the pouch in ice water until cold and keep in the fridge for up to three days.

To regenerate from cold place in the water bath at 88°C for 10 minutes.

Chef's Tip —

Try adding honey, orange, bay leaf, truffle or just plain butter or olive oil to the pouch.

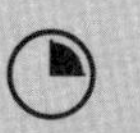
1 hr 20

90°C

Two

Easy

52 Baby Parsnips

INGREDIENTS

1 Bunch of baby parsnips – peeled

1 tbsp Honey

1 tbsp Caster sugar

½ tsp Sea salt

1 tsp Thyme leaves

75ml Duck fat

METHOD

1. Pre-heat your water bath to 90°C.

2. Prepare the parsnips by snipping off the tops and tails – peel and then wash thoroughly.

3. Marinade the parsnips in the thyme, honey, sugar, salt and duck fat.

4. Place the parsnips in a 300cm pouch and vac-seal.

5. Put the pouch into your water bath for 1 hour 20 minutes.

6. Keep checking the water bath to make sure the water is covering the pouch.

7. Remove the parsnips from the pouch, pat dry with kitchen towel and colour in a hot pan.

8. You can place the pouch in ice water until cold and keep in the fridge for up to three days.

To regenerate from cold heat the parsnips in a hot pan.

Chef's Tip –
Sous vide the parsnips in tamarind butter sauce.

45 mins 85°C Two 1 Easy

53

Corn on the Cob

INGREDIENTS

2 Corn on the cobs

110g Unsalted butter

Pinch of sea salt

METHOD

1. Pre-heat your water bath to 85°C.

2. Season the corn with the sea salt.

3. Place the corn in a 300cm pouch, along with the butter and vac-seal.

4. Put the pouch into your water bath for 45 to 55 minutes depending on the size of the corn.

5. Keep checking the water bath to make sure the water is covering the pouch.

6. Remove the cobs from the pouch and serve immediately for lovely crisp corn.

7. You can place the pouch in ice water until cold and keep in the fridge for up to three days.

To regenerate from cold place the pouch in your water bath at 80°C for 15 minutes and serve.

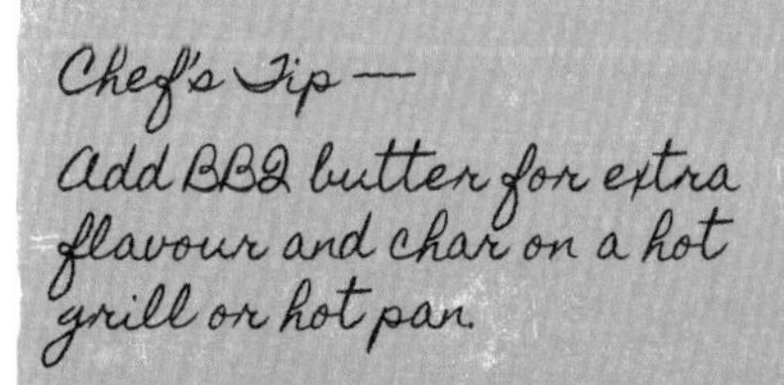

2 hrs

85°C

Four

Easy

54 Fennel

INGREDIENTS

2 Fennel bulbs

1 Glass white wine

1 tsp Sugar

Pinch of star anise powder

½ tsp Sea salt

10 ml White vinegar

Zest of 1½ limes

METHOD

1. Pre-heat your water bath to 85°C.

2. Place the wine, sugar, star anise, salt, vinegar and lime zest in a pan. Bring to a simmer until the ingredients are dissolved. Leave to cool.

3. Remove and discard the outer leaves from the fennel bulbs. Then cut into ½cm slices.

4. Place the fennel slices in a 300cm pouch, along with the cooled liquid and vac-seal. If you have an external vacuum sealer either vacuum seal using a zip lock bag instead or freeze the liquid in an ice cube tray and add to the bag before vacuum sealing with your external vacuum sealer.

5. Put the pouch into your water bath for 2 hours.

6. Keep checking the water bath to make sure the water is covering the pouch.

7. Remove the fennel from the pouch and serve immediately.

8. You can place the pouch in ice water until cold and keep in the fridge for up to three days.

To regenerate from cold heat the fennel in a hot pan.

Chef's Tip —
Finish the fennel bulbs on a grill or in the oven for caramelisation.

15 mins | 85°C | Two | Easy

55 Butter Poached Asparagus

INGREDIENTS

1 Asparagus bunch

50g Butter

½ tsp Salt

50g Truffle butter, truffle oil or freshly grated truffle (optional)

METHOD

1. Pre-heat your water bath to 85°C.

2. Prepare the asparagus by peeling up to the bottom of the spear and place in a pouch along with the peelings.

3. Add the truffle butter and normal butter along with the salt, and vac-seal.

4. Put the pouch into your water bath for 15 minutes.

5. Keep checking the water bath to make sure the water is covering the pouch.

6. Place the pouch in ice water until cold and keep in the fridge for up to three days, or use immediately.

By adding the asparagus peelings – which hold a lot of flavour like a lot of vegetables – it ensures no flavour loss at all.

To regenerate from cold heat the asparagus in a hot pan.

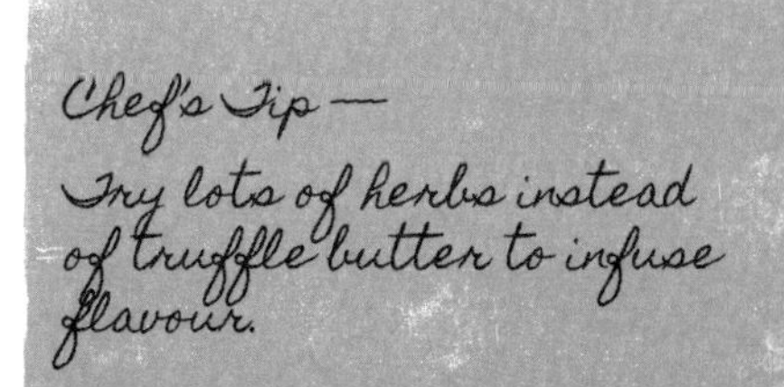

Smoked Cauliflower Cheese Purée

56

Cauliflower and cheese are a classic combination that just works. Smoking the cauliflower enhances the overall flavour and helps to add depth.

INGREDIENTS

1 Cauliflower head

25g Butter

25g Plain flour

600ml Milk

50g Strong cheddar – grated

50g Parmesan – grated

½ tsp English mustard

50ml Olive oil

PolyScience smoking gun

Smoking chips

METHOD

1. Cut the cauliflower into florets and blanch in boiling salted water.

2. Immediately place in ice water to stop the cooking and allow to drain.

3. While the cauliflower is draining, melt the butter in a pan and add flour to make a roux.

4. Cook the roux until it becomes sandy in texture.

5. At this point add the milk gradually until you use it all and the sauce is velvety and smooth.

6. Add all the grated cheese and mustard, check the seasoning is to your taste.

7. Then, marinade the cauliflower florets in olive oil.

8. Place cauliflower florets in an air tight container or glass cloche and smoke using the smoking gun.

9. Leave for between 5 and 10 minutes.

10. Repeat the smoking process 6 or 7 more times. Or more if you want a really smoked flavour.

11. Reheat the cauliflower in the oven until warm and smoke one more time before serving.

Chef's Tip –
Seasoning is important on this dish so be sure to season well.

50 mins
9 times
Four
5
Hard
— Dish Suggestion —
Serve with Cheese Purée and Crispy Sage.

25 mins | 85°C | Two | Easy

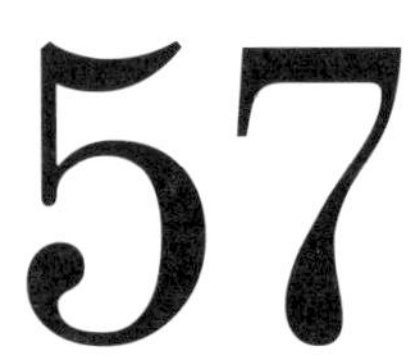

Portobello Mushroom with Garlic

INGREDIENTS

2 Portobello mushrooms – or field mushrooms

1 Thyme sprig

Salt

1 Garlic clove – crushed

50ml Oil or beef fat

METHOD

1. Pre-heat your water bath to 85°C.

2. Peel the skin from the mushrooms and remove the stalks.

3. Season the mushrooms with salt and place in a pouch, along with the thyme, crushed garlic cloves and oil/fat, and vac-seal.

4. Put the pouch into your water bath for 25 minutes.

5. Keep checking the water bath to make sure the water is covering the pouch.

6. Remove the mushrooms and colour in a hot pan serving immediately.

7. You can place the pouch in ice water until cold and keep in the fridge for up to three days.

To regenerate from cold heat the mushrooms in a hot pan.

Chef's Tip –
You can infuse any flavour with the mushroom – try thyme, rosemary or even pesto.

45 mins 85°C Four Easy

58 Pumpkin

INGREDIENTS

1 Small pumpkin

4 Sage sprigs or 12 leaves

1 tbsp Smoked paprika

50g Parmesan —shaved

Salt

METHOD

1. Pre-heat your water bath to 85°C.

2. Peel the pumpkin and remove the seeds, portion into wedges and season with salt.

3. Dust the pumpkin with paprika and place in a pouch, along with the sage, and vac-seal.

4. Put the pouch into your water bath for 45 minutes or 1 hour 30 minutes depending on the size of your pumpkin.

5. Keep checking the water bath to make sure the water is covering the pouch.

6. Remove the pumpkin when tender and colour in a hot pan to caramelise, serving immediately.

7. You can place the pouch in ice water until cold and keep in the fridge for up to three days.

To regenerate from cold heat the pumpkin in a hot pan.

Chef's Tip —
Pumpkin goes really well with orange so why not add marmalade to the pouch.

2½ hrs | 86°C | Two | 2 Easy

59 Beetroot

INGREDIENTS

500g Fresh purple beetroot

50g Caster sugar

1 tsp Thyme leaves

1 tbsp Honey

40ml Raspberry vinegar

METHOD

1. Pre-heat your water bath to 86°C.

2. Wearing gloves, peel the beetroot. Then wash under cold water to avoid staining.

3. Slice the beetroot thinly, about the thickness of a coin.

4. Place in a bowl and add all of the other ingredients. Tossing together to coat the beetroot slices.

5. Place the slices in a pouch, along with any left over liquid and vac-seal.

6. Put the pouch into your water bath for 2 hours 30 minutes.

7. Keep checking the water bath to make sure the water is covering the pouch.

8. Remove the beetroot from the pouch and serve immediately.

9. You can place the pouch in ice water until cold and keep in the fridge for up to five days.

To regenerate from cold heat the beetroot in the oven.

Chef's Tip —
Add a little orange juice and orange zest instead of raspberry vinegar.

1 hr 62°C Four Hard

60 Truffle Poached Egg

INGREDIENTS

30cm Square of cling film

4 Free range eggs

2 Grated truffle

Pinch of Sea salt

5ml Oil

METHOD

1. Pre-heat your water bath to 62°C.

2. Place the cling film piece on top of a cup and press down so the cling film sinks down into the cup.

3. Put the oil in the cling film and rub around to cover the sides, pour out any excess oil.

4. Grate the truffle into the cling film and crack the egg into it as well.

5. Pull up the four corners of the cling film and tie a tight knot that touches the top of the egg.

6. Place the package in your water bath for 1 hour.

7. This time and temperature will create a soft egg yolk and a firmer egg white.

8. After the hour carefully remove the egg and season with salt.

A really fresh egg has a firmer raw egg white which results in a firmer cooked egg.

If the egg is older then the white won't support the yolk in a fixed position. So a fresher egg is best.

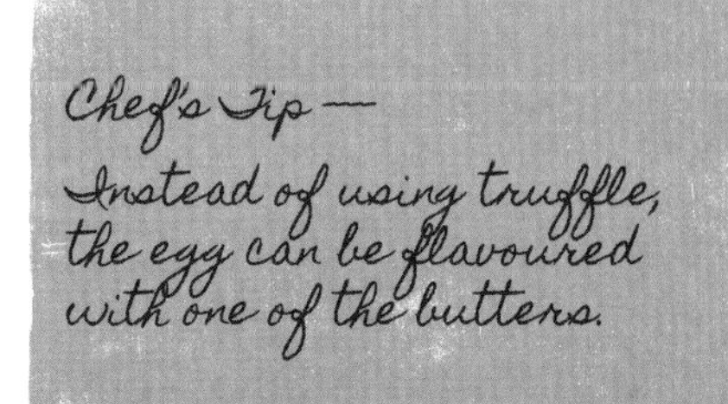

61

Sous Vide Free Range Egg

A sous vide egg is a delight, the grated truffle adds a decadent flavour and works really well with the tender asparagus.

INGREDIENTS

4 Free range eggs — medium size

Sea salt

Pepper

METHOD

1. Pre-heat your water bath to 62°C.

2. Place the eggs in your water bath, just on their own with nothing else, for 1 hour.

3. This time and temperature will create a soft egg yolk and a firmer egg white.

4. Remove the eggs and crack open into a bowl and season.

A really fresh egg has a firmer raw egg white which results in a firmer cooked egg.

If the egg is older then the white won't support the yolk in a fixed position. So a fresher egg is best.

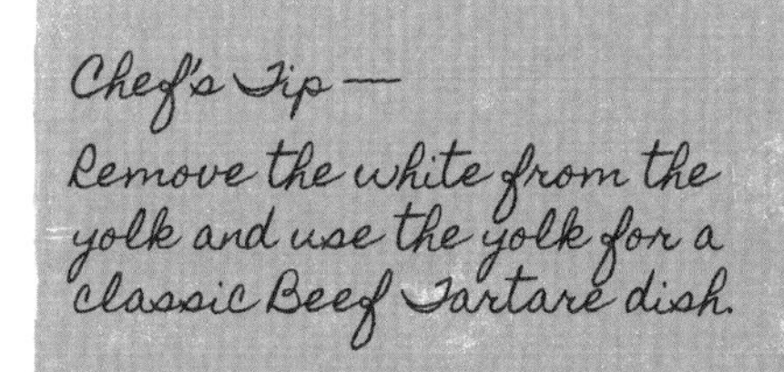

2
1 hr
62°C
Four
Easy
— Dish Suggestion —
Truffle Poached Free Range Egg and Butter Poached Asparagus.

62

Smoked Crème Fraîche and Poached Egg Yolk

Crème Fraîche is widely used to add acidity to soups, sauces or sweet mousses and parfaits. Smoking changes it all together.

INGREDIENTS

200ml Good quality crème fraîche

100g Ceps, or any wild mushroom

4 Eggs

1 Black truffle – grated,
or black truffle oil

Salt

Pepper

PolyScience smoking gun

Applewood smoking chips

METHOD

1. Pre-heat your water bath to 62°C.

2. Place crème fraîche in a small cup or shallow tray, and then under a glass cloche or in an airtight container.

3. Smoke it once and leave for around 10 minutes.

4. Then, stir the crème fraîche making sure the top surface is folded in.

5. Meanwhile place the eggs in the water bath for 1 hour.

6. Repeat the smoking and stirring of the crème fraîche 8 more times.

7. When the crème fraîche is ready, season to taste and add the grated truffle or 2 drops truffle oil and stir in.

8. Colour off the ceps until golden brown in a hot pan.

9. Plate up with a good spoon full of the crème fraîche.

10. Remove the eggs from the water bath, crack open and gently remove the white to reveal the golden yolk and serve.

Chef's Tip —
Add 45 ml of the pickling liquor when placing in the poach to give a pickled/ smoked flavour.

1 hr
62°C
Four
4
Med
— Dish Suggestion —
Smoked Truffled Crème Fraîche, Roasted Ceps and Poached Egg Yolk.

Tangerines, Clementines,
Oranges, Blackberries,
Blueberries, Strawberries,
Pear, Mango, Plums, Peaches,
Rhubarb, Apricots, Apple,
Pineapple, Watermelon
and Gooseberries.

Fruits

All the fruits in this section benefit highly just by being vacuum sealed with other flavours. This is because either soft or hard fruits cell walls can be punctured to allow natural flavour to come out and marinade in their own juices. Or when the cell walls are punctured other flavours can enter and enhance the fruit you want to cook.

Spiced Oranges in Saffron is a great example of this, as the spice, saffron and Cointreau flavours enter the orange, they gently enhance it while being cooked.

3 hrs | 68°C | Four | 2 Easy

63

Spiced Tangerines

INGREDIENTS

6 Tangerines

1 Cinnamon stick

2 Star anise

6 Sage leaves

100g Castor sugar

50ml Whisky

75ml Water

METHOD

1. Pre-heat your water bath to 68°C.

2. Peel and segment the tangerines.

3. With a small knife, clean off all the white pith.

4. In a pan dissolve the sugar, whisky and water. Add the cinnamon stick, star anise and sage to make an infused syrup. Leave to cool.

5. Place the tangerine segments in a pouch, along with the cooled syrup and vac-seal. If you have an external vacuum sealer either vacuum seal using a zip lock bag instead or freeze the syrup in an ice cube tray and add to the bag before vacuum sealing with your external vacuum sealer.

6. Put the pouch into your water bath for 3 hours.

7. Keep checking the water bath to make sure the water is covering the pouch.

8. Remove the tangerine segments from the pouch and serve.

9. You can place the pouch in ice water until cold and keep in the fridge for up to three days.

Chef's Tip —
For a sweeter version, you can poach the fruit in orange juice and thyme.

30 mins | 65°C | Four | 2 Easy

64 Clementines

INGREDIENTS

5 Clementines

Peel of 1 orange

100ml Freshly squeezed orange juice

1 tbsp Sugar

50ml Cointreau

METHOD

1. Pre-heat your water bath to 65°C.

2. Peel the skin and white pith off the clementines and segment.

3. Place the clementine segments in a pouch, along with the rest of the ingredients and vac-seal. If you have an external vacuum sealer either vacuum seal using a zip lock bag instead or freeze the juice in an ice cube tray and add to the bag before vacuum sealing with your external vacuum sealer.

4. Put the pouch into your water bath for 30 minutes.

5. Keep checking the water bath to make sure the water is covering the pouch.

6. Remove the clementine segments from the pouch and serve.

7. You can place the pouch in ice water until cold and keep in the fridge for up to three days.

Chef's Tip —
Use beetroot juice to give great flavour and a two tone colour. Serve with duck for classic Duck a l'orange.

30 mins

70°C

Two

Easy

Spiced Oranges in Saffron

INGREDIENTS

2 Oranges — peeled and sliced

1 Pinch saffron strands

6 Cardamom pods — crushed

2 Bay leaves

1 tbsp Coriander seeds — toasted

50ml Cointreau

METHOD

1. Pre-heat your water bath to 70°C.

2. Place the orange pieces in a pouch, along with the saffron, spices and Cointreau, and vac-seal. If you have an external vacuum sealer vacuum seal using a zip lock bag instead.

3. Put the pouch into your water bath for 30 minutes.

4. Keep checking the water bath to make sure the water is covering the pouch.

5. Remove the oranges from the pouch and serve.

6. You can place the pouch in ice water until cold and keep in the fridge for up to three days.

Chef's Tip —
Add the cooking liquid to a savoury sauce or add 100ml more orange juice and set with gelatine at a ratio of 100ml to 1 leaf for a saffron jelly.

1½ hrs

60°C

Two

Easy

Blackberries

INGREDIENTS

250g Blackberries

50ml Red wine vinegar

60g Castor sugar

2 tsp Hibiscus flowers (optional)

¼ tsp Sea salt

2 Bay leaves

METHOD

1. Pre-heat your water bath to 60°C.

2. Place the red wine vinegar, castor sugar, hibiscus flowers and bay leaves in a pan. Heat gently to dissolve the sugar, then allow to cool.

3. Place the blackberries and sea salt in a pouch, along with the cooled liquid and vac-seal. If you have an external vacuum sealer vacuum seal using a zip lock bag instead.

4. Put the pouch into your water bath for 1 hour 30 minutes.

5. Keep checking the water bath to make sure the water is covering the pouch.

6. Place the pouch in ice water until cold and keep in the fridge for up to three days, or serve immediately.

Chef's Tip —
Replace red wine vinegar with sloe gin or just red wine — add orange zest instead of hibiscus flowers.

1 hr 10 | 60°C | Two | 2 Easy

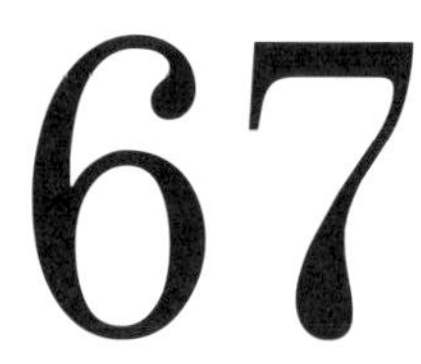

Mulled Blueberries

INGREDIENTS

250g or Punnet of blueberries

500ml Mulled sloe gin — see ***cocktails***

50g Sugar

METHOD

1. Pre-heat your water bath to 60°C.

2. Place all the ingredients in a pouch and vac-seal. If you have an external vacuum sealer vacuum seal using a zip lock bag instead.

3. Put the pouch into your water bath for 1 hour 10 minutes.

4. Keep checking the water bath to make sure the water is covering the pouch.

5. Remove the blueberries from the pouch and serve.

6. You can place the pouch in ice water until cold and keep in the fridge for up to three days.

Chef's Tip —
Make a pickling liquor, vac-seal with the blueberries and sous vide at the same temperature and time.

40 mins | 62°C | Four | Easy

Strawberries

INGREDIENTS

500g Strawberries

2 tbsp Strawberry jam

50g Icing sugar

200ml Sparkling wine

METHOD

1. Pre-heat your water bath to 62°C.

2. Prepare strawberries by removing the green stem – 'hulling' – and cut in half lengthways.

3. Dust the strawberries with icing sugar and place in a pouch.

4. In a pan, make a syrup with the sparkling wine and jam. Allow to cool.

5. Add the cooled syrup to the strawberries and vac-seal. If you have an external vacuum sealer vacuum seal using a zip lock bag instead.

6. Put the pouch into your water bath for 40 minutes.

7. Keep checking the water bath to make sure the water is covering the pouch.

8. Place the pouch in ice water until cold and keep in the fridge for up to three days, or serve immediately.

Chef's Tip –
Try elderflower cordial and black pepper instead of sparkling wine.

Pear

69

The sweet smelling pears, blue cheese and walnuts combine to create some very pleasing flavours and textures. The perfect dish if you can't decide between dessert and cheese.

INGREDIENTS

4 Pears

3 Lavender sprigs – fresh or dried

50g Caster sugar

100ml Fresh pear juice

1 tbsp Honey

METHOD

1. Pre-heat your water bath to 80°C.

2. Peel the pears top to bottom, then cut into 4 length ways.

3. With a knife remove the core, slice the pears and place in a pouch.

4. In a pan place the pear juice, lavender, honey and sugar, bring to a simmer and dissolve the sugar.

5. Once the sugar is dissolved, allow the liquid to cool.

6. Place the sweet smelling liquid in the pouch with the pears and vac-seal. If you have an external vacuum sealer vacuum seal using a zip lock bag instead or freeze the juice in an ice cube tray and add to the bag before vacuum sealing with your external vacuum sealer.

7. Put the pouch into your water bath for between 20 and 30 minutes. This depends on the ripeness of your pears.

8. Keep checking the water bath to make sure the water is covering the pouch.

9. Remove the pears from the water bath and refrigerate for up to five days until required.

Chef's Tip –
Try the pears with red wine, star anise and liquorice sticks with added sugar to form a syrup.

30 mins
80°C
Four
2
Easy
— Dish Suggestion —
Lavender Poached Pears with Blue Cheese, Yoghurt and Walnut Praline.

20 mins 72°C Two Easy

Mango

INGREDIENTS

2 Mangos

150ml Coconut milk

75g Sugar

½ Fresh red chilli — seeds removed

1 tsp Lemongrass — finely chopped

1 tsp Ginger — finely chopped

METHOD

1. Pre-heat your water bath to 72°C.

2. Peel the mangos and cut the four cheeks away from the stone.

3. Place all the remaining ingredients in to a pan, bring to boil to create a syrup. Simmer for 5 minutes.

4. Pass the liquid through a fine strainer or sieve and leave to cool.

5. Put the mango, along with the cooled syrup, in a pouch and vac-seal. If you have an external vacuum sealer vacuum seal using a zip lock bag instead.

6. Put the pouch into your water bath for 20 minutes.

7. Keep checking the water bath to make sure the water is covering the pouch.

8. Place the pouch in ice water until cold and keep in the fridge for up to three days, or serve immediately.

Chef's Tip —
Make a syrup out of lime peel, sugar and water to poach the mango.

35 mins

75°C

Four

Easy

71

Plums with Amaretto and Tarragon

INGREDIENTS

4 Plums – halved, stones removed

Icing sugar to sift

25g Fresh tarragon

50g Castor sugar

1 Pinch sea salt

75ml Amaretto

50ml Water

1 tsp Honey

METHOD

1. Pre-heat your water bath to 75°C.

2. Dust the open side of plums with icing sugar.

3. Then place the plums in a hot non-stick pan to caramelise.

4. Allow the plums to cool and place in a pouch, along with remaining ingredients, and vac-seal. If you have an external vacuum sealer vacuum seal using a zip lock bag instead.

5. Put the pouch into your water bath for 25 to 35 minutes. This depends on the ripeness of your fruit.

6. Keep checking the water bath to make sure the water is covering the pouch.

7. Remove the plums from the water bath and refrigerate until required.

Chef's Tip —
You can freeze the liquid remaining from the pouch creating a plum and amaretto granita.

Peaches and Almond Cream

72

The toasted almonds add an extra bite to this delicious dish, while the cardamom adds an elegant freshness. You will want to keep the liquid for the panna cotta...

INGREDIENTS

5 Peaches

400ml Milk

200g Ground almonds – toasted

150g Sugar

2 Cardamom pods – crushed

4 Leaves gelatine – soaked in water

METHOD

1. Pre-heat your water bath to 80°C.

2. Toast the almonds in a pan.

3. Add the milk, sugar and cardamom pods to the toasted almonds. Infuse the liquid in a pan – *but do not let it boil.* Allow to cool.

4. Remove the stones from the peaches and place in a pouch, along with the cooled liquid, and vac-seal. If you have an external vacuum sealer vacuum seal using a zip lock bag instead.

5. Put the pouch into your water bath for 15 to 20 minutes. This depends on the ripeness of your fruit.

6. Keep checking the water bath to make sure the water is covering the pouch.

7. Remove the peaches from the water bath and refrigerate until required.

8. Pass the remaining liquid through a sieve onto soaked gelatine – allowing the gelatine to dissolve.

9. Pour the mixture into moulds and refrigerate for 4 hours until set.

10. From this, you have created peach and almond panna cotta.

Chef's Tip –
This dish would work just as well with apricots.

20 mins
80°C
Four
3
Med
— Dish Suggestion —
Almond Poached Peaches with Cardamom and Milk Panna Cotta.

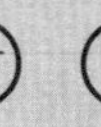

20 mins | 65°C | Four | Easy

Rhubarb Poached with Orange and Champagne

INGREDIENTS

1kg Rhubarb

250g Sugar

200ml Pink Champagne

1 Star anise – crushed to a powder

Zest of 1 orange

METHOD

1. Pre-heat your water bath to 65°C.

2. Peel and chop the rhubarb into 2 inch long by a ¼ inch batons.

3. Warm the Champagne, orange zest, star anise and sugar together allowing the sugar to dissolve. Leave to cool.

4. Place the rhubarb in a pouch, along with the cooled liquid, and vac-seal. If you have an external vacuum sealer vacuum seal using a zip lock bag instead.

5. Put the pouch into your water bath for 15 to 20 minutes. This depends on the ripeness of your rhubarb.

6. Keep checking the water bath to make sure the water is covering the pouch.

7. Remove the rhubarb from the water bath and refrigerate until required.

Chef's Tip –
For Champagne jelly, set the remaining liquid with gelatine with a ratio of 100ml to 1 leaf.

20 mins | 80°C | Four | Easy

Apricots

INGREDIENTS

10 Apricots

250ml Muscat

2 tbsp Honey

1 Vanilla pod – split

1 Rosemary sprig

METHOD

1. Pre-heat your water bath to 80°C.

2. Cut the apricots in half and remove the stones.

3. Place the apricots in a pouch, along with the muscat, honey, vanilla pod and rosemary, and vac-seal. If you have an external vacuum sealer vacuum seal using a zip lock bag instead.

4. Put the pouch into your water bath for between 18 and 20 minutes. This depends on the ripeness of your apricots.

5. Keep checking the water bath to make sure the water is covering the pouch.

6. Remove the apricots from the water bath and refrigerate for up to five days until required.

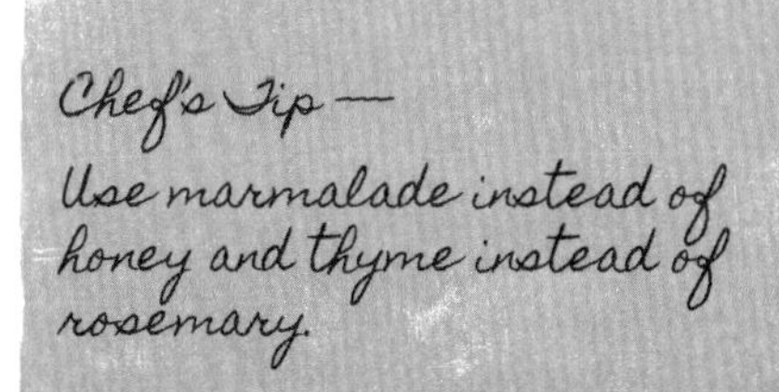

90 secs Two 2 Easy

Pickled Apple

INGREDIENTS

1 Granny Smith apple
— peeled and cored

Pickling Liquor, see ***pickling***

METHOD

1. Peel, core and prepare the apple to the desired size and shape for how you want to present them.

2. Place in a pouch using a ratio of 3 parts apple to 1 part pickling liquor.

3. Vacuum on full compression for 90 seconds.

4. Preserve the apple in your fridge overnight while still sealed in the pouch.

5. The apple can stay in the fridge for between three and five days until needed.

Please note this technique is only applicable for a Chamber Vacuum Sealer.

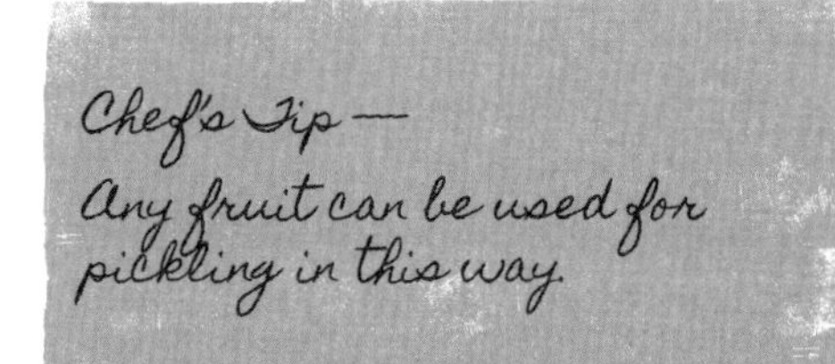

5 hrs | 70°C | Four | Med

Candied Toffee Apple

INGREDIENTS

100g Soft brown sugar

50ml Honey

200ml Dry white wine

4 Granny Smith apples
— peeled and cored

STAGE 1

1. Pre-heat your water bath to 70°C.

2. Melt the sugar and honey in a pan until completely dissolved to a caramel. Keep an eye on it so it doesn't burn.

3. Add the white wine to stop the caramel from cooking.

4. At this stage the caramel will go hard and sticky — turn the heat down until you have a smooth caramel and allow it to cool.

STAGE 2

5. Peel, core and cut the apples into 8 segments.

6. Place the apples in a pouch, along with the cooled caramel, and vac-seal. If you have an external vacuum sealer be vigilant that the caramel does not creep up the bag into the seal. If you see the caramel starting to be sucked towards the machine stop the process immediately. If in doubt use a zip lock bag instead.

7. Put the pouch into your water bath for 5 hours.

8. Keep checking the water bath to make sure the water is covering the pouch.

9. You can keep the pouch in the fridge for up to five days.

Chef's Tip —
You can candy apple using maple syrup or golden syrup depending on flavour required.

77

Pineapple Braised with Rum and Cardamom

Rich, sweet, sticky... sounds perfect doesn't it? The dark rum adds a real kick elevating the pineapple to new heights.

INGREDIENTS

1 Pineapple – peeled

150g Soft brown sugar

1 tsp Cardamom powder

150ml Dark rum

METHOD

1. Pre-heat your water bath to 80°C.

2. Peel the pineapple and make a powder with the brown sugar and cardamom in a pestle and mortar.

3. Rub this powder all over the pineapple.

4. Place the pineapple in a pouch, along with the dark rum, and vac-seal. If you have an external vacuum sealer vacuum seal using a zip lock bag instead.

5. Put the pouch into your water bath for 24 hours.

6. Keep checking the water bath to make sure the water is covering the pouch.

7. Place the pouch in ice water until cold and keep in the fridge for up to three days, or slice and serve immediately.

Chef's Tip –
Chargrill the pineapple when cold or warm straight from the pouch and serve.

24 hrs
80°C
Four
3
Med
— Dish Suggestion —
Rum and Cardamom Braised Pineapple with Fromage Frais Ice Cream.

2 hrs

60°C

Six

Easy

Watermelon

INGREDIENTS

1 Watermelon

200ml Vodka

50g Icing sugar

¼ tsp Sea salt

2 tsp Tarragon – chopped

METHOD

1. Pre-heat your water bath to 60°C.

2. Peel the watermelon and remove all the white pith.

3. Dice into 1cm cubes, discarding any seeds along the way.

4. Dust the watermelon with icing sugar and season with sea salt.

5. Place the watermelon in a pouch, with the vodka and tarragon, and vac-seal. If you have an external vacuum sealer vacuum seal using a zip lock bag instead.

6. Put the pouch into your water bath for 2 hours.

7. Keep checking the water bath to make sure the water is covering the pouch.

8. Place the pouch in ice water until cold and keep in the fridge for up to three days, or serve immediately.

Chef's Tip —
Match the watermelon with strawberry juice, light ale or orange liquor.

 8 hrs  58°C  Two  Easy

Gooseberries

INGREDIENTS

500g Gooseberries

150ml Elderflower cordial

250ml White wine

250g Sugar

Zest of ½ orange

Juice of 1 lime

1 Vanilla pod – split

METHOD

1. Pre-heat your water bath to 58°C.

2. Remove the brown stem from the top of the gooseberries.

3. Add the wine, zest, lime juice, vanilla, elderflower cordial and sugar to a pan and bring to a simmer. Heat until the sugar has dissolved.

4. Place the gooseberries in a pouch, along with the syrup, and vac-seal.
If you have an external vacuum sealer vacuum seal using a zip lock bag instead.

5. Put the pouch into your water bath for between 6 to 8 hours. This depends on the ripeness of your gooseberries.

6. Keep checking the water bath to make sure the water is covering the pouch.

7. Place the pouch in ice water until cold and keep in the fridge for up to three days, or serve immediately.

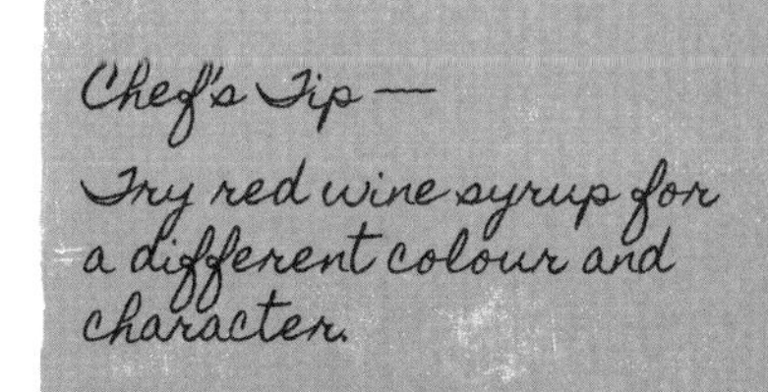

Custard, Toast, Anise,
Walnut, Balsamic, Sesame,
Truffled Honey, Chocolate,
Gingerbread and Thyme.

Ice Cream

Not just for savoury, the precise nature of the sous vide technique means with a bit of imagination it's more than capable of producing fine desserts too.

It's a perfect way of infusing flavours — just by adding thyme with an ice cream base adds a really fresh flavour.

80

Custard for Ice Creams

Custard for ice creams or just for saucing can be tricky at the best of times if you haven't got a temperature probe or sugar thermometer. This is where sous vide comes in...

INGREDIENTS

500ml Cream

500ml Milk

12 Egg yolks

200g Sugar

2 Vanilla pods
– split and deseeded

This technique helps to bring the custard mixture up to the pasteurisation temperature, killing harmful bacteria in the egg yolk 82°C.

If you were to make custard in a pan, you'd have to decide when to take it off, usually 3–6°C before it's ready as the residual heat could 'scramble' your custard. If you haven't got a temperature probe then this is a hard task to master for the amateur cook.

So, cooking the custard base in the water bath ensures even cooking all through the mixture and knowledge that pasteurisation has been achieved. After this its just a simple case of chilling and churning.

METHOD

1. Pre-heat your water bath to 82°C.

2. Mix the egg yolks with sugar and whisk together, place in a pouch with the milk, cream and vanilla pods and vac-seal.

3. Put the pouch into your water bath for 1 hour 30 minutes.

4. During the cooking time, remove the pouch and massage or agitate the custard mix 3 or 4 times to ensure even cooking.

5. Place the pouch in ice water for 15 minutes and reserve ready to churn.

1½ hrs
82°C
Eight
3
Med

2½ hrs

82°C

Eight

Med

81 Toast Ice Cream

INGREDIENTS

500ml Milk

600ml Cream

10 Slices of bread

12 Egg yolks

150g Sugar

150g Soft butter

2 Pinches of salt

STAGE 1

1. Pre-heat your water bath to 82°C.

2. Toast off the bread and place in a pouch with the milk and cream, vac-seal.

3. Put the pouch into your water bath for 1 hour.

4. After this time, remove the pouch and pass the contents through a sieve.

STAGE 2

5. Whisk the sugar with the yolks, soft butter and salt.

6. Place the mixture in a pouch with the sieved liquid and vac-seal.

7. Put the pouch into your water bath for 1 hour 30 minutes at 82°C, agitating three times.

8. Pass the mixture off and churn immediately or refrigerate ready to churn later.

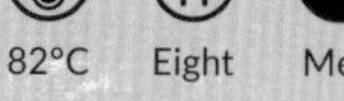

2½ hrs | 82°C | Eight | Med

Anise Ice Cream

INGREDIENTS

500ml Milk

600ml Cream

25 Star anise – crushed

1 Vanilla pod – split

12 Egg yolks

150g Sugar

STAGE 1

1. Pre-heat your water bath to 82°C.

2. Crush the star anise and place in a pouch with the milk and cream, vac-seal.

3. Put the pouch into your water bath for 2 hours.

4. After this time, remove the pouch and pass the contents through a sieve.

STAGE 2

5. Whisk the sugar with the yolks and place in a pouch with the sieved liquid and vanilla pod, vac-seal.

6. Put the pouch into your water bath for 30 minutes at 82°C, agitating three times.

7. Pass the mixture off and churn immediately or refrigerate ready to churn later.

2 hrs 82°C Eight Med

83

Walnut Ice Cream

INGREDIENTS

800ml Milk

1 litre Cream

500g Walnuts
– chopped and lightly roasted

20 Egg yolks

300g Sugar

STAGE 1

1. Pre-heat your water bath to 82°C.

2. Toast off the walnuts and place in a pouch with the milk and cream, vac-seal.

3. Put the pouch into your water bath for 1 hours 30 minutes.

4. After this time, remove the pouch and pass the contents through a sieve.

STAGE 2

5. Whisk the sugar with the yolks and place in a pouch with the sieved liquid, vac-seal.

6. Put the pouch into your water bath for 30 minutes at 82°C, agitating three times.

7. Pass the mixture off and churn immediately or refrigerate ready to churn later.

You can save the walnuts and fold through the churning ice cream.

1½ hrs 82°C Eight Med

84 Balsamic Ice Cream

INGREDIENTS

500ml Milk

600ml Cream

50g Glucose syrup

140ml Good quality balsamic

12 Egg yolks

120g Sugar

METHOD

1. Pre-heat your water bath to 82°C.

2. Place all the ingredients except the balsamic in a pouch and vac-seal.

3. Put the pouch into your water bath for 1 hour 30 minutes.

4. Then, pass the contents of the pouch through a fine sieve.

5. Slowly whisk in the balsamic and allow to cool.

6. Reserve until cool then churn.

It is important that the balsamic gets added after the custard is cooked because it could split the raw egg and cream if added at the start.

1 hr 55 | 82°C | Eight | 3 Med

85

Sesame Ice Cream

INGREDIENTS

500ml Milk

600ml Cream

200g Toasted sesame seeds

20ml Sesame oil

12 Egg yolks

200g Sugar

100g Light tahini paste

STAGE 1

1. Pre-heat your water bath to 82°C.

2. Place the sesame seeds and sesame oil in a pouch with the milk and cream, vac-seal.

3. Put the pouch into your water bath for 1 hour 30 minutes.

4. After this time, remove the pouch and pass the contents through a sieve.

STAGE 2

5. Whisk the sugar, yolks and tahini paste and place in a pouch with the sieved liquid, vac-seal.

6. Put the pouch into your water bath for 25 minutes at 82°C, agitating three times.

7. Pass the mixture off and churn immediately or refrigerate ready to churn later.

86

Truffled Honey Ice Cream

INGREDIENTS

500ml Milk

600ml Double cream

100g Honey

50g Truffled honey

12 Egg yolks

100g Sugar

METHOD

1. Pre-heat your water bath to 82°C.

2. Whisk the sugar with the yolks, place in a pouch, along with the remaining ingredients, and vac-seal.

3. Put the pouch into your water bath for 1 hour 30 minutes, agitating three times.

4. Place the pouch in ice water until cold and reserve ready to be chilled.

Truffle honey is widely available at delicatessens up and down the country or at more high end supermarkets.

The Truffle adds a decadent background flavour without over powering the ice cream and brings balance.

87

Chocolate Ice Cream

INGREDIENTS

750ml Milk

750ml Double cream

450g Dark chocolate, 100% cocoa

15 Egg yolks

100g Sugar

METHOD

1. Pre-heat your water bath to 82°C.

2. Whisk the sugar with the yolks, adding the milk and double cream to it whisking as you do.

3. Place in a pouch, along with the chocolate, and vac-seal.

4. Put the pouch into your water bath for 1 hour 30 minutes, agitating three times.

5. Pass the mixture off and refrigerate ready to churn later.

1½ hrs

82°C

Eight

Med

Gingerbread Ice Cream

INGREDIENTS

500ml Yoghurt

500ml Double cream

1 tsp Grated ginger

½ tsp Ginger powder

250g Gingerbread – crumbled up

12 Egg yolks

300g Sugar

METHOD

1. Pre-heat your water bath to 82°C.

2. Place all the ingredients in a large pouch, except the gingerbread crumbs, and vac-seal.

3. Put the pouch into your water bath for 1 hour 30 minutes, agitating three times.

4. Remove from the pouch and pass through a fine sieve into a container and allow to cool.

5. When cool, add the gingerbread crumbs and churn.

2 hrs | 82°C | Eight | Med

Thyme Ice Cream

INGREDIENTS

500ml Milk

500ml Double cream

10 Thyme sprigs

12 Egg yolks

190g Sugar

STAGE 1

1. Pre-heat your water bath to 82°C.

2. Add the milk, cream and thyme to a pouch and vac-seal.

3. Put the pouch into your water bath for 1 hour 30 minutes.

4. After this time, remove the pouch and pass the contents through a sieve.

STAGE 2

5. Whisk the sugar with the yolks and place in a pouch with the sieved liquid, vac-seal.

6. Put the pouch into your water bath for 30 minutes at 82°C, agitating three times.

7. Pass the mixture off and refrigerate ready to churn later.

Bellini, Mulled Wine,
Eggnog, Snowball, Sloe Gin
and Blackberry Cocktail,
Passion Fruit Mojito and
Long Island Iced Tea.

Cocktails

The process of the cocktail is for alcohol to extract essences from anything it comes into contact with without losing any alcohol from itself. Some cocktails or alcohol essences require days or weeks for the alcohol to absorb and carry the flavour of what it has come into contact with. For instance fruit flavoured brandys or limoncello can take weeks if left at room temperature.

You can use heat to speed up the process but then flavour and alcohol is lost through evaporation. This is where sous vide comes in — you can speed up the process of flavour absorption without flavour loss and evaporation. This can be used to make alcoholic flavour, sealed in a bag in the fridge, ready to be made into a cocktail when you desire.

90

Bellini

STAGE 1 INGREDIENTS

5 Peaches

50g Castor sugar

STAGE 2 INGREDIENTS

2 Peaches

Champagne

Icing sugar

STAGE 1

1. Pre-heat your water bath to 90°C.

2. Burn the peach skin with a blow torch or under a grill to blacken the skin.

3. Then rub the skin off with a towel.

4. Cut the peaches in half and remove the stone.

5. Place the peaches in a pouch and vac-seal. If you have an external vacuum sealer vacuum seal using a zip lock bag.

6. Now, put the pouch in the water bath and for 45 minutes, or until the peaches are fully soft.

7. Remove the peaches from the pouch and blend to a purée and put to one side.

STAGE 2

8. Peel the peaches as described in stage 1 and cut in half.

9. Slice the peaches ½cm thick and dust with icing sugar.

10. Place the peaches in a large pouch and compress for 99 seconds.

11. Leave in the pouch until needed.

12. Place the purée in a glass and top with the diced up compressed peaches.

13. Finish with Champagne.

2 hrs  85°C  Two  Med

91 Mulled Wine

INGREDIENTS

1L Red wine

2 Cinnamon sticks

1 tbsp Cloves

1 tbsp All Spice

1 Orange rind – remove white pith

1 Lemon rind – remove white pith

6 tbsp Brown sugar

1 Nutmeg – grated

METHOD

1. Pre-heat your water bath to 85°C.

2. Place the sugar in a pan and start to caramelise, add the rest of the ingredients and allow to bubble until the sugar is dissolved together with the wine and spices.

3. Remove from the heat, allow to cool then place in a pouch and vac-seal. If you have an external vacuum sealer vacuum seal using a zip lock bag.

4. Now, put the pouch in the water bath for between 1 and 2 hours.

5. Remove the liquor from the pouch and strain off.

6. Serve straight away or refrigerate until needed.

92

Eggnog

INGREDIENTS

1L Milk

6 Eggs

50g Castor sugar

1 Vanilla pod – split

200ml Brandy – good quality

1 Nutmeg – grated

METHOD

1. Pre-heat your water bath to 82°C.

2. Mix all the ingredients in a pouch and vac-seal on full compression. If you have an external vacuum sealer vacuum seal using a zip lock bag.

3. Place in the water bath for 1 hour.

4. Halfway through the cooking, remove the pouch and massage in your hands to ensure all the liquid is being evenly dispersed. Put the pouch back in the water bath.

5. Repeat this process after a further 15 minutes and again when the hour is up.

6. Remove the liquid from the pouch and strain through a sieve into a glass and finish with freshly grated nutmeg.

7. You can refrigerate for up to three days until required.

Snowball

Make a Snowball by adding to the Eggnog recipe.

INGREDIENTS

50ml Eggnog

50ml Lime juice

Lemonade

METHOD

1. Shake the eggnog and lime juice together.

2. Pour over ice in a highball glass.

3. Top up with lemonade or use soda water for a less sweet version.

2 hrs | 58°C | Two | 2 Easy

93

Sloe Gin and Blackberry Cocktail

INGREDIENTS

1 Punnet of blackberries

500ml Sloe gin

500ml Blackberry liquor

½ Lemon — juiced

6 Juniper berries — crushed

6 tbsp Hibiscus flowers — dried (optional)

1 Clove

4 tbsp Sugar stock, see ***pickling***

METHOD

1. Pre-heat your water bath to 58°C.

2. Place all ingredients in a large pouch and fully compress. If you have an external vacuum sealer vacuum seal using a zip lock bag.

3. Now, put the pouch in the water bath for 2 hours.

Make sure the bag is fully submerged under the water level.

4. Remove the pouch from the water bath and place in ice water for 20 minutes.

5. Strain off the liquid through a cheesecloth or fine sieve and keep to one side.

6. When required pour the cocktail over crushed ice and garnish with sous vide blackberries.

94 Passion Fruit Mojito

INGREDIENTS

500ml Dark rum

6 tsp Muscovado sugar

½ Bunch of mint

280ml Passion fruit purée

10 Lime leaves

METHOD

1. Pre-heat your water bath to 58°C.

2. Place all the ingredients in a large pouch and fully compress. If you have an external vacuum sealer vacuum seal using a zip lock bag.

3. Now, put the pouch in the water bath for 2 hours.

Make sure the bag is fully submerged under the water level.

4. Remove the pouch from the water bath and place in ice water for 20 minutes.

5. Strain off the liquid through a cheesecloth or fine sieve and keep to one side.

6. Or mix with 50ml soda water with a small amount of ice and crush into a cocktail beaker.

7. Shake well and serve.

2 hrs

58ºC

Four

Easy

Target Temperature

MEAT

Beef, lamb and pork.

Rare:	120°F	49°C
Medium rare:	134°F	56.5°C
Medium:	140°F	60°C
Medium well:	150°F	65.5°C
Well:	160°F	71°C +

POULTRY

Chicken and turkey.

White meat (all poultry)

Medium:	140–146°F	60–63°C

Dark meat (all poultry)

Medium:	176°F	80°C

FISH

Rare:	116°F	47°C
Medium rare:	126°F	52°C
Medium:	140°F	60°C

VEGETABLES AND FRUITS

183–190°F 84–87°C

Note: Raw or unpasteurised food must never be served to highly susceptible immune compromised individuals.

Food should not be kept between 41°F/5°C and 130°F/54.5°C for longer than four hours.

Cooking Times and Temperatures

Minimum/maximum cooking times are for foods starting at refrigerator temperature. Thickness measurement refers to thickness of vacuum sealed pouch.

MEAT

Beef or lamb, tender cuts.
Tenderloin, sirloin, ribeye or t-bone steaks, lambchops.

FOOD	THICKNESS	TEMP	MIN TIME	MAX TIME
Tender beef, lamb	1"/25mm	134°F/56.5°C +	1 hr	4 hrs
Tender beef, lamb	2"/50mm	134°F/56.5°C +	2 hrs	4 hrs

Beef or lamb, tougher/leaner cuts.
Roast, ribs, brisket, flat-iron steak, grass-fed cuts, leg of lamb, game.

FOOD	THICKNESS	TEMP	MIN TIME	MAX TIME
Roast, leg of lamb	2.75"/70mm	134°F/56.5°C +	10 hrs	24–48 hrs
Spare ribs	2"/50mm	176°F/80°C	24 hrs	48–72 hrs
Flank and brisket	1"/25mm	134°F/56.5°C +	8–10 hrs	24–30 hrs
Game	1"/25mm	134°F/56.5°C +	8–10 hrs	12–24 hrs

Pork, tender cuts.
Tenderlion, baby back ribs.

FOOD	THICKNESS	TEMP	MIN TIME	MAX TIME
Tenderloin	1.5"/38mm	134°F/56.5°C +	90 mins	6–8 hrs
Baby back ribs		165°F/74°C +	4–8 hrs	12 hrs

MEAT

Pork, tougher cuts.
Chops, roast, spare ribs.

FOOD	THICKNESS	TEMP	MIN TIME	MAX TIME
Pork chops	1"/25mm	134°F/56.5°C +	2–4 hrs	6–8 hrs
Pork chops	2"/50mm	134°F/56.5°C +	4–6 hrs	8–10 hrs
Pork roast	2.75"/70mm	160–176°F 71–80°C	12 hrs	30 hrs
Spare ribs	2.75"/70mm	160–176°F 71–80°C	12 hrs	30 hrs

POULTRY

FOOD	THICKNESS	TEMP	MIN TIME	MAX TIME
Chicken breast, bone in	2"/50mm	146°F/63.5°C +	2.5 hrs	4–6 hrs
Chicken breast, boneless	1"/25mm	146°F/63.5°C +	1 hr	2–4 hrs
Chicken leg/thigh		160°F/71°C +	4 hrs	6–8 hrs
Split game hen	2.75"/70mm	160°F/71°C +	6 hrs	8 hrs
Turkey/duck leg		176°F/80°C +	8 hrs	10 hrs
Confit	2.75"/70mm	176°F/80°C +	8 hrs	18 hrs
Duck breast	1"/25mm	134°F/56.5°C +	2.5 hrs	6–8 hrs

FISH AND SEAFOOD

FOOD	THICKNESS	TEMP	MIN TIME	MAX TIME
Lean fish	½"/12.5mm	Desired serving	30–40 mins	†
Lean fish	1"/25mm	Desired serving	40–50 mins	†
Lobster	1"/25mm	140°F/60°C	45 mins	†
Scallops	1"/25mm	140°F/60°C	40–60 mins	†
Shrimp	Large/jumbo	140°F/60°C	30 mins	†

VEGETABLES

Root vegetables.

FOOD	THICKNESS	TEMP	MIN TIME	MAX TIME
Beets, carrots, celery, parsnips, potato, turnips	2"/50mm	183°F/84°C	1–2 hrs	4 hrs

Tender vegetables.

FOOD	THICKNESS	TEMP	MIN TIME	MAX TIME
Asparagus, broccoli, cauliflower, corn, aubergine, fennel, green beans, onions, peas, squashes	2"/50mm	183°F/84°C	45 mins	1½ hrs

FRUITS

Firm fruits.

FOOD	THICKNESS	TEMP	MIN TIME	MAX TIME
Apple, pear	2"/50mm	183°F/84°C	45 mins	2 hrs

Soft fruits.

FOOD	THICKNESS	TEMP	MIN TIME	MAX TIME
Peach, apricot, plum, mango, papaya, nectarine, strawberry	2"/50mm	183°F/84°C	30 mins	1 hr

EGGS

Chicken, large (when cooked in shell, do not vacuum seal in pouch)

COOK	QUANTITY	TEMP	MIN TIME	MAX TIME
Soft, in shell — quick	1-12	167°F/75°C	15 mins	18 mins
Soft, in shell — slow	1-12	146°F/63.5°C	45 mins	1½ hrs
Hard, in shell	1-12	160°F/71°C	45 mins	1½ hrs
Scrambled	5	167°F/75°C	20 mins	†
Pasteurised, in shell	1-12	135°F/57°C	1¼ hrs	2 hrs

† Longer cooking times may result in excessively soft texture.

Index